LES FILLES DU ROI

Les Filles du Roi
A musical

Book & lyrics by
Corey Payette & Julie McIsaac

Music by
Corey Payette

Les Filles du Roi
first published 2019 by Scirocco Drama
An imprint of J. Gordon Shillingford Publishing Inc.

Scirocco Drama Editor: Glenda MacFarlane

Cover design by Doowah Design

Author photo of Corey Payette by Nadya Kwandibens
Author photo of Julie McIsaac by Jane Weitzel
Cover photo by Markian Tarasiuk
Production photos by Tim Matheson

Printed and bound in Canada on 100% post-consumer recycled paper.
We acknowledge the financial support of the Manitoba Arts Council and The Canada Council for the Arts for our publishing program.

Licensing Inquiries, please contact:
Playwrights Guild of Canada
401 Richmond Street West, Suite 350
Toronto, Ontario
M5V 3A8
416-703-0201
info@playwrightsguild.ca

Library and Archives Canada Cataloguing in Publication

Title: Les Filles du Roi : a musical / book & lyrics by Corey Payette & Julie McIsaac ; music by Corey Payette.
Names: Payette, Corey, 1987- author. | McIsaac, Julie, 1981- author.
Description: A play. | Text in English, French and Kanien'kéha (Mohawk).
Identifiers: Canadiana 20190168684E | ISBN 9781927922545 (softcover)
Classification: LCC PS8631.A932 F55 2019 | DDC C812.6—dc23

J. Gordon Shillingford Publishing
P.O. Box 86, RPO Corydon Avenue, Winnipeg, MB Canada R3M 3S3

For Mabel and Marguerite

Corey Payette

Corey Payette is proud of his Oji-Cree heritage from Northern Ontario, and has worked as a playwright, actor, composer, and director across Canada. He is the Artistic Director of Urban Ink (Vancouver, BC), was an Artist-in-Residence with English Theatre at Canada's National Arts Centre, and is the founder of Raven Theatre (Vancouver, BC), which focuses on new works by Indigenous artists. Corey has worked as an Artistic Associate with The Indigenous Cycle at the National Arts Centre, an investigation into the broad spectrum of the Indigenous body of work being created within Canada's borders. This cycle resulted in the creation of a new department of Indigenous Theatre at the National Arts Centre.

As a musical theatre creator, Corey's musical *Children of God* (book/music/lyrics and direction) has won numerous awards and has had three national tours: The Cultch (Vancouver), National Arts Centre–English Theatre (Ottawa), Citadel Theatre (Edmonton), Western Canada Theatre (Kamloops), Segal Centre (Montreal), Vernon Performing Arts Centre, Capitol Theatre (Nelson), Key City Theatre (Cranbrook), and the Surrey Arts Centre. *Les Filles du Roi* (music and direction, co-book/lyrics), written in English, French, and Kanien'kéha (Mohawk), was commissioned by Fugue Theatre and co-produced by Raven Theatre, Urban Ink, and The Cultch in 2018. *Sedna* (creation, music, and direction) was commissioned by Urban Ink and co-produced at Caravan Farm Theatre in 2018. Corey's next musicals have been commissioned by Bard on the Beach (Vancouver), Musical Stage Company (Toronto), and the Stratford Festival (Stratford).

The album recording *The Music from Les Filles du Roi,* the *Children of God* published script, the album recording *Corey Payette – The Music from Children of God,* and the Piano/Vocal songbook are available at www.coreypayette.com

Julie McIsaac

Julie is of French, Scottish/Irish, and Scandinavian ancestry, and grew up in Ontario, on the territory of the Huron-Wendat, Haudenosaunee, and Anishinabek Nations. A multidisciplinary performer and director of theatre and opera, she is a graduate of Carleton University, the Canadian College of Performing Arts, and the University of York (UK). Directing credits include the international tour of Sum Theatre's *My Rabbi*, the British Columbia premiere of *The Exquisite Hour* (Playhouse Fringe award), and the multiple award-winning *Poly Queer Love Ballad* by Sara Vickruck & Anais West. She has appeared on stages throughout Western Canada, including the Citadel, Arts Club, Bard on the Beach, Pacific Theatre, the Belfry Theatre, Firepot Performance (formerly Twenty Something Theatre), Fugue Theatre, Carousel Theatre, and the Chemainus Theatre Festival. She is a four-time Jessie nominee, an Ovation award winner, Associate Artist of Firepot Performance, a founding member of the Honest Fishmongers, and a past Artist-in-Residence at Pacific Opera Victoria. She is also the playwright, composer-arranger, music director, and co-sound designer of *The Out Vigil* (Firepot Performance) for which she shared a Jessie award with Jay Clift. www.juliemcisaac.com

Nia:wen / Merci / Thank You

Cecelia King, Darren Bonaparte, Iawenta's Mabel White, JoAnn Swamp, Kahentawaks Perkins, Kahniehtiio Horn, Kathy Herne, Michel Cadieux, Pascal Perron, Sue Ann Swamp, Tekonwakwenni Nanticoke, Marshall McMahen, Patrice Bowler, Lisa Goebel, Alex Schoen, Anita Rochon, Anna Kuman, Barbara Adler, Caitlyn Hayes, Cate Richardson, Dawn Brennan, Deneh'Cho Thompson, Elliot Vaughan, Estelle Shook, Evan Frayne, Geneva Perkins, Heather Redfern, JD Derbyshire, Jeff Gladstone, Jesse Martyn, Johnny Trinh, Julie Trépanier, Karliana DeWolff, Kevin Loring, Laura Di Cicco, Laura Ross, Lindsay Warnock, Lucy Sim, Mara Gottler, Maria Jose Herrera, Megan Stewart, Melanie Thompson, Michael Creber, Michael James Park, Robyn Wallis, Sidney Klips, and to the community members of Akwesasne.

The creators are grateful to all the funders of this work: City of Vancouver, BC Arts Council, Vancouver Foundation, and especially to the Canada Council New Chapter Grant.

This is one of the 200 exceptional projects funded through the Canada Council for the Arts' New Chapter program. With this $35M investment, the Council supports the creation and sharing of the arts in communities across Canada.

Ce projet est l'un des 200 projets exceptionnels soutenus par le programme Nouveau chapitre du Conseil des arts du Canada. Avec cet investissement 35 M$, le Conseil des arts appuie la création et le partage des arts au cœur de nos vies et dans l'ensemble du Canada.

Canada Council for the Arts Conseil des arts du Canada

New Chapter 2017 and Beyond Nouveau Chapitre 2017 et au-delà

Director / Composer / Co-Book / Lyricist's Statement

My great-grandmother Mabel moved from Caughnawaga (Kahnawake) Mohawk Territory on the south shore of the St. Lawrence River, across from Montreal, to Northern Ontario in the early 1900s. She spoke English and French but Kanien'kéha (Mohawk) was her first language. She was discriminated against for being Indigenous and never taught Kanien'kéha to her children; the language was lost in our family. In fact she shared very little with them about their own language or culture. Now with the support of the Native North American Travelling College in Akwesasne, we not only received some teachings of the Kanien'kéha language but also some of the worldview that is embedded within this complex language. With only two generations between us, I feel like this reclaiming of Indigenous language through *Les Filles du Roi* is part of a larger story that will resonate with many young Indigenous peoples who are on this same path.

We are using this musical as a vehicle to tell the story through the perspective of generations of silenced Indigenous peoples whose stories have gone unheard by the mainstream. It challenges the history we've been told and asks us to reconsider the narrative. Stories are powerful, they shift how we see the world, and our history has been shaped through a predominantly white male perspective. Much of our work in *Les Filles* is about Indigenizing the narrative because these perspectives are missing. Even when we spoke to Indigenous scholars in Akwesasne, many of their sources were through the same white lens we were looking to subvert.

In addition to the Indigenous perspective being missing, we found few perspectives of *les filles* who had come over. Our work has been about feminizing this history through the eyes of these women. The chorus sheds light on the aspects of truth that are lost by having such a narrow perspective of these complex histories. We now have the opportunity to share all the complexities of these women told through the extraordinary talents of our women's chorus, who represent what our community is comprised of today. It has been 352 years since the time our story is set, and in that time we have experienced the loss of matriarchy, which was the way of governance in the Kanien'kehá:ka nation at the time of our story. This is why the women needed to play all characters in this story – because they have all felt the impacts of the loss of this Indigenous worldview. I hope it serves as a reminder of what was once present on this land and of what we still could be.

I never met Great-Grandmother Mabel, but I know she would be proud that we are reclaiming Kanien'kéha in this way. We will speak our language again, language will bring songs again, songs will bring dances again, and even if we have to create the story anew, these stories will remind us of who we have always been.

All my relations,

Corey Payette
Director / Composer / Co-book / Lyricist – *Les Filles du Roi*
Artistic Director of Urban Ink
Founder of Raven Theatre

Co-Book / Lyricist's Statement

When I first learned about the historical *filles du roi,* I was in Grade 8 at L'École Saint-Joseph in Penetanguishene, Ontario. I felt a fierce kinship with these girls, likely because I was the same age as many of them would have been when they left France to become young wives (and mothers) in the "new world." I've never stopped wondering about these girls; why they went, what they left behind, and what really happened when they arrived. The documented history is narrow, paternalistic, wholly unsatisfying. Statistics are available – passenger manifests, marriage certificates, census records – but what about the lived experiences of these women? Yes, they were population-boosting possessions of the patriarchy. But what did they themselves think, dream, feel?

This gap in the narrative is what prompted me to talk to Laura Di Cicco, Artistic Director of Fugue Theatre, about a show that would give voice to *les filles*. At the same time, I knew there were / are other perspectives missing from accounts of our nation's history. These young women arrived as products and agents of a system, a system that was bent on destroying the way of life of the Indigenous people of this continent, a system that has resulted in centuries of oppression, violence, and erasure. A system that is ongoing, and will continue to harm, unbalance, and separate us; unless we take action, together.

As I grappled with this, and Laura asked me about potential collaborators, I knew that I needed to talk to Corey Payette. I am so grateful that Corey was inspired to take part, and in such a significant way. And I'm thankful for all that this show has taught us, both artistically and personally. We've uncovered parts of our own identities, family histories we might never have known if not for the pull of the questions at the heart of this piece. I am fortunate to have grown up surrounded by the vivacious and tenacious women of my French-Canadian family: my *mémère* Simone, my mother Jeanne, and my eight *ma tantes* Marie, Irène, Avela, Madeleine, Anne, Gisèle, Yvette, and Bonita. Now I know that all of us are descended from *fille du roi* Marguerite Bulté, who married in 1670 and lived to be 85 years old.

What if my ancestor only survived because of the kindness and generosity of Corey's ancestors? What if settlers had allowed themselves to be changed by genuinely listening to, and learning from, the Indigenous people of this land? What if we settlers committed to doing this now? What if Western European patriarchy wasn't our default modality? What if it went without saying that women's voices and bodies are to be honoured, revered, and respected?

On behalf of Corey and myself – Nia:wen (thank-you) to all the people who have believed in this work. To Laura at Fugue for commissioning the seed of an idea and supporting us over all these years; to Dawn, JD, and Samantha at Urban Ink; to The Cultch and Raven Theatre; and to this remarkable company of artists for bringing *Les Filles du Roi* to life.

Julie McIsaac
Co-Book/Lyricist of *Les Filles du Roi*

Production History

Les Filles du Roi had its world premiere on May 17, 2018 at the York Theatre in Vancouver, produced by Fugue Theatre & Raven Theatre in association with Urban Ink and The Cultch. *Les Filles du Roi* was commissioned by Fugue Theatre and received development support from Fugue Theatre, Raven Theatre, Urban Ink, Caravan Farm Theatre, the Native North American Travelling College (Akwesasne), and/et Centre d'interprétation du site archéologique Droulers-Tsiionhiakwatha (Saint-Anicet, Québec).

Original Cast:

Kaitlyn Yott .... Kateri
Julie McIsaac .... Marie Jeanne Lespérance
Raes Calvert .... Jean-Baptiste / Fight Captain
Laura Di Cicco .... Madame Savoie
Andrew Cohen .... Clarke
Chelsea Rose .... Clan Mother / Chorus
Kayla Dunbar .... Lise Anne / Chorus
Synthia Yusuf .... Chorus
Lisa Goebel .... Chorus / Dance Captain
Cecilly Day .... Chorus
Merewyn Coreau .... Chorus

Musicians:

Rachel Kiyo Iwaasa (Piano)
Molly MacKinnon (Violin)
John Kastelic (Viola)
Rebecca Wenham (Cello)

Creative Team:

Director / Composer / Co-book / lyrics: Corey Payette

Co-book / lyrics: Julie McIsaac

Production Design (Set / Costume / Props): Marshall McMahen

Music Director: Rachel Kiyo Iwaasa

Co-Orchestrators: Elliot Vaughan & Martin Reisle

Lighting Design: Jeff Harrison

Sound Design: Kyra Soko

Beadwork Design: Konwahonwá:wi Stacey

Movement Director: Patrice Bowler

Co-Fight Directors: Mike Kovac & Ryan McNeil Bolton

Kanien'kéha Language Teacher: Iawenta's Mabel White

Kanien'kéha Language Consultants and Translators: Kathy Herne, JoAnn Swamp, Cecelia King, Sue Ann Swamp & Tekonwakwenni Nanticoke

Associate Movement Director & Dance Captain: Lisa Goebel

Assistant Director: Emilie Leclerc

Stage Manager: Ashley Noyes

Assistant Stage Manager: Melanie Thompson

Surtitlist: Sarah Jane Pelzer

Production Team:

Managing Director: Dawn Brennan
Creative Producer: JD Derbyshire
Production Manager: Adrian Muir
Sound Board Operator: Kyra Soko
Head of Wardrobe: Stephanie Kong
Cutter: Victoria Klippenstein
Seamstresses: Megan Veaudry,
Jessica Oostergo, Oriana Camporese
Wardrobe Breakdown: Bunny Meugens
Props Master: Sharon Zimmerman

In 2017, *Les Filles du Roi* received a workshop from Fugue Theatre at the Arts Club Theatre in Vancouver, BC. The following ensemble was involved in that development: Lisa Goebel, Lucinda Sim, Anna Kuman, Chelsea Rose, Synthia Yusuf, Laura Di Cicco, Kayla Dunbar, and Laura Ross.

Corey Payette .... Composer, Director, co-book/lyrics
Julie McIsaac .... Co-book/lyrics
Patrice Bowler .... Movement Direction
Marshall McMahen .... Set & Costume Design
Jeff Harrison .... Lighting Design
Elliot Vaughan............................... Orchestration

In 2016, *Les Filles du Roi* received a workshop and public presentation from Fugue Theatre at the Annex Theatre in Vancouver, BC.

Workshop Cast:

Kaitlyn Yott..Kateri

Cate Richardson........ Marie Jeanne Lespérance

Raes Calvert ....Jean-Baptiste / Fight Captain

Laura Di Cicco .... Madame Savoie

Jeff Gladstone..Clarke

Patrice Bowler
Karliana Dewolff
Maria Jose Herrera
Sidney Klips
Geneva Perkins
Lindsay Warnock.......................................Chorus

Creative Team:

Director / Composer / Co-book / lyrics:
Corey Payette

Co-book / lyrics: Julie McIsaac

Lighting Design: Marshall McMahen

Music Director / piano: Caitlyn Hayes

Stage Manager: Melanie Thompson

Workshops were held in previous years produced by Fugue Theatre featuring the following casts and creative teams: Anita Rochon, Deneh'Cho Thompson, Evan Frayne, Jesse Martyn, Kevin Loring, Laura Di Cicco, Robyn Wallis, and Kaitlyn Yott.

Les Filles du Roi: a musical by Corey Payette & Julie McIsaac. Directed by Corey Payette, Production Design (Set / Costume / Props) by Marshall McMahen, Lighting Design by Jeff Harrison. A Fugue Theatre / Raven Theatre production in association with Urban Ink and the Cultch. Actors: Kayla Dunbar, Chelsea Rose, Cecilly Day, Julie McIsaac, Lisa Goebel, Synthia Yusuf, and Merewyn Comeau.

Les Filles du Roi: a musical by Corey Payette & Julie McIsaac. Directed by Corey Payette, Production Design (Set / Costume / Props) by Marshall McMahen, Lighting Design by Jeff Harrison. A Fugue Theatre / Raven Theatre production in association with Urban Ink and the Cultch. Actors: Raes Calvert and Kaitlyn Yott.

Les Filles du Roi: a musical by Corey Payette & Julie McIsaac. Directed by Corey Payette, Production Design (Set / Costume / Props) by Marshall McMahen, Lighting Design by Jeff Harrison. A Fugue Theatre / Raven Theatre production in association with Urban Ink and the Cultch. Actors: Julie McIsaac and Raes Calvert.

Les Filles du Roi: a musical by Corey Payette & Julie McIsaac. Directed by Corey Payette, Production Design (Set / Costume / Props) by Marshall McMahen, Lighting Design by Jeff Harrison. A Fugue Theatre / Raven Theatre production in association with Urban Ink and the Cultch. Full Acting Company: Raes Calvert, Lisa Goebel, Kayla Dunbar, Synthia Yusuf, Andrew Cohen, Kaitlyn Yott, Laura Di Cicco, Cecilly Day, Chelsea Rose, Merewyn Comeau, and Julie McIsaac.

Les Filles du Roi: a musical by Corey Payette & Julie McIsaac. Directed by Corey Payette, Production Design (Set / Costume / Props) by Marshall McMahen, Lighting Design by Jeff Harrison. A Fugue Theatre / Raven Theatre production in association with Urban Ink and the Cultch. Actor: Kaitlyn Yott.

Les Filles du Roi: a musical by Corey Payette & Julie McIsaac. Directed by Corey Payette, Production Design (Set / Costume / Props) by Marshall McMahen, Lighting Design by Jeff Harrison. A Fugue Theatre / Raven Theatre production in association with Urban Ink and the Cultch. Actors: Raes Calvert, Kaitlyn Yott, and Julie McIsaac.

Les Filles du Roi: a musical by Corey Payette & Julie McIsaac. Directed by Corey Payette, Production Design (Set / Costume / Props) by Marshall McMahen, Lighting Design by Jeff Harrison. A Fugue Theatre / Raven Theatre production in association with Urban Ink and the Cultch. Actors: Cecilly Day, Lisa Goebel, Merewyn Comeau, Julie McIsaac, Synthia Yusuf, Chelsea Rose, and Kayla Dunbar.

World Premiere Opening Night. Photo taken May 17, 2018. Left to right: Sarah Jane Pelzer, Laura Di Cicco, Synthia Yusuf, Ashley Noyes, Rachel Iwaasa, Lisa Goebel, Melanie Thompson, Cecilly Day, Marshall McMahen, Molly MacKinnon, Corey Payette, Kaitlyn Yott, Rebecca Wenham, Julie McIsaac, Raes Calvert, John Kastelic, Chelsea Rose, Merewyn Comeau, Kyra Soko, Kayla Dunbar, and Andrew Cohen.

Characters

KATERI .... 12 years old. Kanien'kehá:ka (Mohawk). She is Bear Clan, and in line to be Clan Mother when she's older. Sister of Jean-Baptiste.

MARIE JEANNE .... 16 years old. French. A *fille du roi* from a merchant family in Paris, recently arrived in Nouvelle-France. Sister of Lise Anne.

JEAN-BAPTISTE .... 18 years old. Kanien'kehá:ka (Mohawk). He is Bear Clan. A trapper-trader who speaks several languages, well known throughout the territory. Older brother of Kateri.

MADAME SAVOIE .... 36 years old. French. Religious. A fervent royalist, living in Nouvelle-France.

CLARKE .... 27 years old. An Englishman in Ville-Marie. The youngest son from an upper-class British family. The same actor doubles as SAILOR and PRIEST.

LISE ANNE .... 14 years old. French. A *fille du roi*. Marie Jeanne's sister.

CLAN MOTHER .... Kanien'kehá:ka (Mohawk). She is Bear Clan. Aunt of Kateri and Jean-Baptiste; the sister of their mother.

WOMEN'S CHORUS .... An ensemble of young women who populate the world of the story, moving between various characters and locations: *les filles du roi*; sailors on the ship; soldiers in the fort; family members back in France; women of the Longhouse; colonists, farmers, ancestors.

Song List

LES FILLES DU ROI
Full Company

IAKOIANEH (Clan Mother)
Kateri

PRIÈRE EN MARCHANT (Walking Prayer)
Full Company

L'ESPACE (Space)
Marie Jeanne and *Filles*

BEYOND THE WALLS
Marie Jeanne and Jean-Baptiste

SICKNESS
Full Company

WINTER
Instrumental

COLD ISN'T PERMANENT
Jean-Baptiste and Kateri

QUI ME SAUVERA? (Who Will Save Me?)
Marie Jeanne

SICKNESS (reprise)
Madame Savoie and Chorus

SKÉN:NEN KOWA (Great Peace)
Clan Mother and Chorus

WE COULD BE
Marie Jeanne and Jean-Baptiste

TOSAH ENSATERENAIEN (Don't Pray to Your God)
Kateri and Marie Jeanne

FINALE
Full Company

Setting

Story takes place between Summer 1665 and Summer 1666;
Various locations on unceded Kanien'kehá:ka territory
in and around Ville-Marie (later Montréal).

A Note About the Text

An ellipsis … indicates a trail-off of speech.

Text in CAPS is sung.

Text in open brackets ( ) indicates English translation of
Kanien'kéha or French words / phrases.

Scene 1

LES FILLES DU ROI

Late summer, 1665. Dawn. By the river. Far off in the distance, a church bell tolls. JEAN-BAPTISTE enters, carrying a pile of furs. KATERI follows behind him.

KATERI: Raktsi:ah *(big brother).* You'll need help carrying these to the fort.

JEAN-BAPTISTE: Careful, that's our best pelt. It'll trade well.

KATERI: I can help you paddle across.

JEAN-BAPTISTE: You're here to help out in camp. The fort is no place for you.

KATERI: I want to see their big canoes.

JEAN-BAPTISTE: It's dangerous.

KATERI: Then you shouldn't go alone.

JEAN-BAPTISTE: I've made the trip many times.

KATERI: With the other men, never on your own.

JEAN-BAPTISTE: It's not a safe place for you. There's sickness in the fort.

KATERI: There's sickness in our village too. Iakoianeh *(Clan Mother)* says I need to learn everything I can. How can I do that from a camp across the river? I won't go in the fort. I'll watch the canoe and this stuff.

JEAN-BAPTISTE: *(Pause.)* It's hard work. If you come, no complaining.

KATERI: I never complain.

JEAN-BAPTISTE: And you'll do whatever I say.

KATERI: Yeah, except for when you're being a grump. Then you're on your own.

JEAN-BAPTISTE: Eh kati tho. *(So be it.)*

Across the river by the French fort, a sailing ship approaches. MADAME SAVOIE greets les filles du roi.

MADAME SAVOIE: VOILÀ NOTRE GLOIRE LA NOUVELLE-FRANCE
FILLETTES, REGARDEZ CE PAYS
C'EST DIEU LE SEIGNEUR QUI L'A CRÉÉ
REGARDEZ CE ROYAUME, IL NOUS L'A DONNÉ
(Look, see our glory, New France
My girls, look at this land
It's the Lord God who created it
Look at the kingdom He has given us)

RENDEZ GRÂCE À LOUIS QUI VOUS A CHOISI
POUR PEUPLER SA CHÈRE COLONIE
VOICI VOTRE DESTIN, CETTE TERRE FÉCONDE
BIENVENUE AU NOUVEAU MONDE
(Give thanks to Louis who has chosen you
To populate His dear colony
Here is your destiny, this fertile land
Welcome to the New World)

MADAME SAVOIE: Catherine Joly.

SAILOR: Dysenterie. *(Dysentery.)*

MADAME SAVOIE: Apolline Lemoyne.

SAILOR: Fièvre. *(Fever.)*

MADAME SAVOIE: Lise Anne Lespérance.

SAILOR: Décédée. *(Deceased.)*

MADAME SAVOIE: La cause? *(The cause?)*

SAILOR: Noyade. *(Drowning.)*

MADAME SAVOIE: Marie Jeanne Lespérance.

On the deck of the ship arriving in harbour, MARIE JEANNE stands at the bow, looking out to the new world, seeing all the people gathered to welcome them.

MARIE JEANNE: LA GLOIRE D'LA FRANCE ET LE BON DIEU
C'EST POUR LUI QU'NOUS SOMMES TOUTES ICI
ET POUR LOUIS LE ROI SOLEIL
QUI M'A CHOISI
(The glory of France and our merciful Lord
We're all here for Him
And for Louis the Sun King
Who has chosen me)

TRAVERSER A FAILLI ME TUER
MALGRÉ LES TEMPÊTES, LA MALADIE
JE SUIS ICI, NOUS SOMMES ICI
LES FILLES DU ROI
(The crossing nearly killed me
But in spite of all the storms and sickness
I'm here, we're all here
The daughters of the King)

LES FILLES join MARIE JEANNE at the bow of the ship. They look out to the shore and to the people welcoming them.

MARIE JEANNE & FILLES:

LES FILLES DU ROI
LES FILLES DU ROI
(The daughters of the King
The daughters of the King)

On the shore by the French fort, KATERI and JEAN-BAPTISTE set up their trading post. During the following, KATERI keeps stopping her work to look at the settlers; as he works, JEAN-BAPTISTE weaves in front and around her, trying to block her view and keep her focused.

KATERI: Takerihón:nien ne taiakwathà:ren. *(Teach me how to talk to them.)*

JEAN-BAPTISTE: I'll do the talking. You watch and listen.

KATERI: How do I listen if I don't know what they're saying?

JEAN-BAPTISTE: You don't need to know what they're saying.

KATERI: But I need to trade with them.

JEAN-BAPTISTE: I trade, you guard the canoe. That's the deal, remember?

KATERI: Iah, iah tetkaie:ri'. *(No, that's not right.)* I said watch the canoe – and I can watch from here.

JEAN-BAPTISTE:

IAH TESATERIÉNTARE. TAKWÉTAK NE ONEN
ENKÌ:RON ENKOIA'TAKENHA
(You cannot know the harm they do.
Believe me when I say that I'm protecting you)

KATERI:

YOU KNOW I CAN BE BRAVE TOO
LET ME GO AND I'LL SHOW YOU

I'll talk to the women.

JEAN-BAPTISTE: There are no women.

KATERI: Iasatkátho raktsi:ah! *(Look, big brother!)* A big canoe! From across the sea – satkato, satkato, satkato *(look, look, look)*!

MARIE JEANNE & FILLES:

UNE DERNIÈRE FOIS J'DIS AU REVOIR
J'M'APPRÊTE À RENCONTRER MA GLOIRE
J'RETOURNERAI JAMAIS À PARIS
L'AVENIR SE TROUVE ICI
(One final goodbye
Getting ready to go meet my glory
I'll never again go back to Paris
The future is here before me)

(Overlapping.) J'AI MA CASSETTE: UNE PAIRE DE BAS
UNE COIFFE, UN BONNET, UN MOUCHOIR
DES GANTS, DES ÉPINGLES, DES AIGUILLES
DU FIL ET DES CISEAUX
(I've got my trousseau: a pair of socks,
A comb, a bonnet, a handkerchief
Gloves, some pins, some needles
Some thread and scissors)

KATERI: ARE THOSE GIRLS THE SAME AS ME?
BROTHER, LET'S GO DOWN AND SEE

JEAN-BAPTISTE: STAY BY MY SIDE, WE'LL WATCH FROM HERE
YOU FOOLISH GIRLS, SO MUCH TO FEAR

MADAME SAVOIE & PRIEST:

HABITANTS, REGARDEZ LES BELLES FILLES DU ROI
LES BIJOUX DE NOTRE PATRIE
FILLETTES, CHOISISSEZ-VOUS UN BON MARI
DONNEZ-VOUS AU NOM DE LOUIS
(Habitants, look; the pretty daughters of the King
The jewels of our homeland
Girls, choose yourselves a good husband
Give yourselves in the name of Louis)

MARIE JEANNE & FILLES:

LES VOILÀ, LES CÉLIBATAIRES
UNE CENTAINE D'HOMMES, QUE DOIS-JE FAIRE?
MON MARIAGE EST IMMINENT
MAIS QUI CHOISIR, COMMENT?
(Look, there they are, the bachelors
A hundred men, what should I do?
My marriage, it's imminent
But who to choose, and how?)

C'EST POUR LOUIS, LA FRANCE, ET LE SEIGNEUR
LOUIS, LA FRANCE, ET LE SEIGNEUR
LOUIS, LA FRANCE, ET LE SEIGNEUR
JE FERAI MON DEVOIR
(I'm doing this for Louis, for France, and the Good Lord
For Louis, France, and the Good Lord
For Louis, France, and the Good Lord
I will do my duty)

JEAN-BAPTISTE: *(Overlapping.)*
LES FILLES DU ROI WHY, ARE YOU HERE?
PLEASE JUST GO HOME, OR DISAPPEAR

KATERI: *(Overlapping.)*
LES FILLES DU ROI, CAN YOU HEAR ME?
WHAT IS IT LIKE ACROSS THE SEA?

ALL: LES FILLES DU ROI
LES FILLES DU ROI
BIENVENUE AU NOUVEAU MONDE
(The daughters of the King
The daughters of the King
Welcome to the New World)

LES FILLES come ashore. The colonists gather, and a PRIEST blesses the young women. KATERI approaches them, watching closely. JEAN-BAPTISTE rushes towards her.

JEAN-BAPTISTE: Kateri.

KATERI: Tóte'k, raktsi:ah. *(Quiet, big brother.)* They're in ceremony.

JEAN-BAPTISTE: *(Pulling her close to him.)* I told you to stay by my side.

KATERI: You told me to watch; I'm watching. What's that, hanging from their sleeves?

JEAN-BAPTISTE: La dentelle. *(Lace.)*

KATERI: How do they garden in those dresses?

JEAN-BAPTISTE: They don't.

MADAME SAVOIE spots JEAN-BAPTISTE and KATERI. JEAN-BAPTISTE moves to stand in front of KATERI, trying to block her from view.

MADAME SAVOIE: She:kon, monsieur. *(Hello, sir.)*

JEAN-BAPTISTE: She:kon, Madame Savoie. *(Hello, Madame Savoie.)*

MADAME SAVOIE: Nahò:ten iontakiats? *(What is her name?)*

KATERI: Kateri iónkiats. Okní:se? *(My name is Kateri. And you?)*

MADAME SAVOIE: Sehiá:ra'k monsieur ia taonton iaontawéia'te tsík sans qu'elle soit baptisée. *(I will remind you, sir; she is not welcome in the fort until she is baptized.)*

KATERI: Oh nahò:ten kénton? *(What does that mean?)*

JEAN-BAPTISTE: Tha'tesató:tat. *(Behave – be quiet.)*

The PRIEST concludes his blessing and MADAME SAVOIE steps forward, presenting KATERI to LES FILLES. JEAN-BAPTISTE watches tensely.

MADAME SAVOIE: Cette jeune sauvage est la raison pour laquelle le bon Dieu nous a révélé ce pays. Nous devons la sauver – et pour faire cela, il faut purifier l'esprit ainsi que le corps. La conversion des sauvages, pour la gloire de notre Seigneur Jésus Christ. *(This young savage is the reason the Good Lord revealed this land to us. We need to save her – and to do that, we need all of you to be pure in both mind and body. The conversion of the savages, for the glory of our Lord Jesus Christ.)*

MADAME SAVOIE, the PRIEST, and LES FILLES make the sign of the cross. MADAME SAVOIE turns back to KATERI.

Wahs. *(Go away.)*

JEAN-BAPTISTE guides KATERI back towards the trading post.

KATERI: Raktsi:ah, tell her I like the sleeves of her dress.

JEAN-BAPTISTE: Tohsa satá:ti. *(No talking.)*

MADAME SAVOIE: *(To LES FILLES.)* Suivez-moi à l'Hôtel-Dieu. Nous nous débarrasserons de la saleté du navire, d'accord? *(Follow me to the Hotel-Dieu. We'll rid ourselves of that filth from the ship, yes?)*

MADAME SAVOIE exits with MARIE JEANNE and LES FILLES.

At the trading post, JEAN-BAPTISTE is swiftly packing up their furs.

KATERI: Takrori nahoten wà:ehron. Karíwes iakó:thare. *(Tell me what she said. She talked a long time.)*

JEAN-BAPTISTE: Help me with the furs, konkén:'a *(sister).* Madame Savoie told the girls they were here to save us.

KATERI: Save us? They don't even know us.

JEAN-BAPTISTE: Everything works differently here. Their world is not ours.

KATERI: The wampum shows us together, our nations side by side. Sha'té:ioht. *(It is the same on one side as the other side.)*

JEAN-BAPTISTE: Í:iah thaón:ton. *(It's not possible.)*

IAKOIANEH (Clan Mother)

KATERI: Katkek iakoianeh enkáton. *(I'll be Clan Mother one day.)* How can I do what's best if you won't tell me about their ways? I need to learn how to talk to them.

JEAN-BAPTISTE: A good Clan Mother doesn't go around telling everyone she will be Clan Mother. She is humble; maybe you need learn more of that.

KATERI: YOU WEREN'T THERE WHEN MOTHER DIED
I WAS RIGHT THERE AT HER SIDE
WHEN SHE SAID TO ME

FROM NOW ON, MY KATERI
EVERYWHERE YOU LOOK, YOU'LL SEE
THINGS STRANGE, THINGS CHANGE

THERE'S DANGER THERE
JUST LIKE EVERYWHERE
BUT YOU WILL SEE MORE THAN YOU KNOW
THAT A FIRE IN YOU IS STARTING TO GROW,
TO GROW

JEAN-BAPTISTE: Tho, tho. *(Fine.)* I'll teach you some of the language. *(Pause.)* It's been a long day, let's start tomorrow.

He exits. KATERI calls after him.

KATERI: Nià:wen kowa, raktsi:ah. *(Thank-you so much, big brother.)*
I HAVE AKSOTHA'S *(my grandmother's)* EYES
SHINING DARK AND DEEPLY WISE
SHE SAID THEY'VE CHOSEN ME

NOW I KNOW WHAT I MUST BE
NOW I KNOW THERE'S CHANGE, I SEE
OUR CLAN, OUR PEOPLE, NEED ME

THERE'S DANGER THERE
JUST LIKE EVERYWHERE
BUT I CAN DO MORE THAN YOU KNOW
A FIRE IN ME IS STARTING TO GROW

THERE'S DANGER THERE
JUST LIKE EVERYWHERE
BUT I CAN DO MORE THAN YOU KNOW
A FIRE IN ME STARTING TO GROW, TO GROW

TOKA IAKOIANEH ENKÁTON
TOKA IAKOIANEH EN
TAKERIHÓN:NIEN
TOKA IAKOIANEH EN
(If I will be Clan Mother
If I am Clan Mother
You need to teach me
If I am Clan Mother)

THERE'S DANGER THERE
JUST LIKE EVERYWHERE
BUT I WILL DO MORE THAN YOU KNOW
THIS FIRE IN ME IS STARTING TO GROW

AND STILL I'LL GO
THERE'S MORE TO KNOW
TAKERIHÓN:NIEN *(You need to teach me)*

She exits.

Scene 2

That evening, at the Hôtel-Dieu. MADAME SAVOIE is assessing LES FILLES, inspecting each girl behind a curtain, then dividing them into two groups.

MADAME SAVOIE: Prochaine. *(Pause.)* Prochaine! Comment vous appelez-vous?

MARIE JEANNE: Marie Jeanne.

MADAME SAVOIE: Nom de famille, idiote. *(Last name, you idiot.)*

MARIE JEANNE: Marie Jeanne Lespérance.

MADAME SAVOIE: Âge? *(Age?)*

MARIE JEANNE: Seize ans. *(Sixteen years.)*

MADAME SAVOIE: Lieu de naissance? *(Place of birth?)*

MARIE JEANNE: Paris.

MADAME SAVOIE: Just what we need. Another city girl who's never worked a day in her life. Behind the curtain.

MARIE JEANNE: The nuns checked, before we left La Rochelle. I go to mass every day, Madame. I pray every night.

MADAME SAVOIE: On the chair.

MARIE JEANNE goes behind the curtain, MADAME SAVOIE follows. MARIE JEANNE steps up onto the chair. MADAME SAVOIE passes her hand up under MARIE JEANNE's skirts. A moment, then she withdraws her hand and comes out from behind the curtain.

As I expected. *(Making a note on her paper.)* Stand over there, please.

MARIE JEANNE: On the ship, the sailors… They would only give us fresh water if we…

MADAME SAVOIE: Have you bled since then?

MARIE JEANNE: Yes.

MADAME SAVOIE: Good.

MARIE JEANNE: What happened on the ship wasn't my fault.

MADAME SAVOIE: The best you can hope for is a man who doesn't beat you.

(To all.) Bread and water, then upstairs to bed.

LES FILLES exit. MARIE JEANNE starts following them off, then turns back.

MARIE JEANNE: Is the water here safe to drink?

MADAME SAVOIE: We add vinegar, as a precaution.

MARIE JEANNE: On the ship, the water was rancid. The last week, there were girls dying every day.

MADAME SAVOIE: You survived. Give thanks to God for your good fortune.

MADAME SAVOIE leaves. At a loss, MARIE JEANNE kneels and begins to pray.

PRIÈRE EN MARCHANT
(Walking Prayer)

MARIE JEANNE:
JE VOUS SALUE, MARIE
JE VOUS SALUE, MARIE PLEINE DE GRÂCE
LE SEIGNEUR EST AVEC VOUS
VOUS ÊTES BÉNIE ENTRE TOUTES LES
  FEMMES
ET JÉSUS, LE FRUIT DE VOS ENTRAILLES
EST BÉNI, SAINTE MARIE MÈRE DE DIEU
PRIEZ POUR NOUS, MARIE
PAUVRES PÉCHEURS
MAINTENANT ET À L'HEURE DE NOTRE
  MORT

(Hail Mary
Hail Mary, full of grace
The Lord is with thee
Blessed art thou among women
And Jesus, the fruit of thy womb
Is blessed, Holy Mary, Mother of God
Pray for us, Mary
Poor sinners
Now and in the hour of our death)

Early morning. JEAN-BAPTISTE and KATERI are on their way back to the fort.

JEAN-BAPTISTE: Un. *(One.)*

KATERI: Uh.

JEAN-BAPTISTE: Satkato. *(Look.)* Un.

KATERI: Un.

JEAN-BAPTISTE: Ioianére. *(Good.)*

KATERI: Nahoten ne ó:ia. *(Now the next part.)*

JEAN-BAPTISTE: Thok nikon. *(That's the only part.)*

KATERI: That's it? Un? That's Atsi'tsiaká:ion *(Sky Woman)* who came first? Un?

JEAN-BAPTISTE: Hen. *(Yes.)* Kiorohsaka *(the white men)* don't know of Atsi'tsiaká:ion *(Sky Woman)*. Un is… It's a number and that's all.

KATERI: I don't understand.

JEAN-BAPTISTE: It just means one.

He hides a coin in his hand.

Iah thè:nen. *(None.)*

He reveals the coin.

Énska. *(One.)* Un.

KATERI: Thok nikon? *(That's it?)*

JEAN-BAPTISTE: Thok nikon. *(That's it.)*

KATERI: Un. Un un un.

JEAN-BAPTISTE: Ioianére. *(Good.)*

KATERI: Now Atsi'tsiaká:ion's *(Sky Woman's)* daughter and the twin babies. How do they say the twins?

JEAN-BAPTISTE: Deux. *(Two.)*

KATERI: Deux. *(Two.)*

JEAN-BAPTISTE: (*He points to himself.*) Un. *(He indicates them both.)* Deux.

KATERI: Un. (*One.*) Deux. *(Two.)* And when the birds put Atsi'tsiaká:ion *(Sky Woman)* in the middle of The Great Turtle's back? Ahsen? *(Three?)*

JEAN-BAPTISTE: Trois. *(Three.)*

KATERI: Twa.

JEAN-BAPTISTE: Trrrrrrois.

She tries to roll the 'r' without much success –

KATERI: Trrrrrrrrr… O tsi wentóre. *(That's hard.)*

JEAN-BAPTISTE: Then you'll have to keep practising.

KATERI: If I say it well, can I make a trade tomorrow?

JEAN-BAPTISTE: Satewéienst ne kawennasón:'ah. *(Learn the language first.)*
WAY HI OH WAY HI OH HI WAY YAH YAH
WAY HI OH WAY HI OH HI WAY YAH-HA YAH
(Overlapping.) WAY HI OH WAY HI OH HI WAY YAH YAH
WAY HI OH WAY HI OH HI WAY YAH-HA YAH

During the following, MADAME SAVOIE and LES FILLES enter and walk behind MARIE JEANNE, along a path to the fort that

JEAN-BAPTISTE and KATERI are walking. MADAME SAVOIE chooses a farmer to introduce to one FILLE; they pair up and continue walking, arm in arm.

MARIE JEANNE, MADAME SAVOIE, PRIEST & CHORUS:
(Overlapping.) JE VOUS SALUE, MARIE
JE VOUS SALUE, MARIE PLEINE DE GRÂCE
LE SEIGNEUR EST AVEC VOUS
VOUS ÊTES BÉNIE ENTRE TOUTES LES FEMMES
ET JÉSUS, LE FRUIT DE VOS ENTRAILLES
EST BÉNI, SAINTE MARIE MÈRE DE DIEU
PRIEZ POUR NOUS, MARIE
PAUVRES PÉCHEURS
MAINTENANT ET À L'HEURE DE NOTRE MORT…
(Hail Mary
Hail Mary, full of grace
The Lord is with thee
Blessed art thou among women
And Jesus, the fruit of thy womb
Is blessed, Holy Mary, Mother of God
Pray for us, Mary
Poor sinners
Now and in the hour of our death…)

During the following, JEAN-BAPTISTE and KATERI continue their journey to the fort. MARIE JEANNE is drawn to a farmer and begins talking to him, but is pulled away by MADAME SAVOIE, who remains at her side, brushing off men, preventing MARIE JEANNE from interacting with them. Instead, MADAME SAVOIE introduces the men to other filles. One settler gives money to MADAME SAVOIE, in exchange for access to a woman. Another couple pairs up and are married by the PRIEST.

JEAN-BAPTISTE & KATERI:

(Overlapping.) WAY HI OH WAY HI OH HI WAY YAH YAH
WAY HI OH WAY HI OH HI WAY YAH-HA YAH
WAY HI OH WAY HI OH HI WAY YAH YAH
WAY HI OH WAY HI OH HI WAY YAH-HA YAH

MARIE JEANNE, MADAME SAVOIE, PRIEST & CHORUS:

(Overlapping.) JE VOUS SALUE, MARIE
JE VOUS SALUE, MARIE PLEINE DE GRÂCE
LE SEIGNEUR EST AVEC VOUS
VOUS ÊTES BÉNIE ENTRE TOUTES LES FEMMES
ET JÉSUS, LE FRUIT DE VOS ENTRAILLES
EST BÉNI, SAINTE MARIE MÈRE DE DIEU
PRIEZ POUR NOUS MARIE
PAUVRES PÉCHEURS
MAINTENANT ET À L'HEURE DE NOTRE MORT...
(Hail Mary
Hail Mary, full of grace
The Lord is with thee
Blessed art thou among women
And Jesus, the fruit of thy womb
Is blessed, Holy Mary, Mother of God
Pray for us, Mary
Poor sinners
Now and in the hour of our death...)

MARIE JEANNE is left alone. Unmarried.

PRIEZ POUR NOUS, MARIE
PAUVRES PÉCHEURS
MAINTENANT ET À L'HEURE DE NOTRE MORT...
(Pray for us, Mary
Poor sinners
Now and in the hour of our death...)

JEAN-BAPTISTE and KATERI exit, as do MADAME SAVOIE and the PRIEST.

LES FILLES: AHHHH.

Scene 3

Fall. LES FILLES transform into SOLDIERS and begin chopping wood, sharpening axes, and polishing boots; they are at work building barracks, a trading post nearby.

MARIE JEANNE is working at an outdoor kitchen on the shores of the river; stoking the fire, preparing and serving food. The SOLDIERS ogle and leer at MARIE JEANNE and other passing women, catcalling and making rude gestures. A fight breaks out between two of the men.

CLARKE watches the scene, his eyes on MARIE JEANNE.

CLARKE:

JE VOUS SALUE, MARIE
JE VOUS SALUE, MA CHÈRE MARIE JEANNE
AFIN D'ÊTRE AVEC VOUS…
UNE FEMME BÉNIE PARMI TOUS LES HOMMES
CE MOMENT, LE FRUIT DE VOS ENTRAILLES
ME BÉNI, SAINTE MARIE MÈRE DE DIEU
PRIEZ POUR MOI, MARIE
PAUVRE PÉCHEUR
MAINTENANT ET À L'HEURE DE NOTRE MORT
PRIEZ POUR MOI, MARIE
PAUVRE PÉCHEUR
MAINTENANT ET À L'HEURE DE NOTRE MORT
(I salute you, Marie
I salute you, my dearest Marie Jeanne
In order to be with you…
A woman blessed among all the men
This moment, the fruit of your loins
Is blessing me, Holy Marie, Mother of God
Pray for me, Marie
A poor sinner

Now and in the hour of our death
Pray for me, Marie
A poor sinner
Now and in the hour of our death)

CLARKE: Ça sent bon. *(Smells good.)*

MARIE JEANNE: Le pain est frais, on vient tout juste de le sortir du four. *(The bread's fresh from the ovens.)*

CLARKE: Un paradis terrestre. C'est combien? *(Heaven on earth. How much?)*

MARIE JEANNE: Quatre deniers pour la soupe. Cinq avec du pain. *(Four pence for the soup. Five with bread.)*

CLARKE: Y-a-t'il autre chose au menu? *(Anything else on the menu?)*

MARIE JEANNE: La soupe elle est très bonne, monsieur. Un petit avant-goût, peut-être? *(The soup is very good, monsieur. Would you like a little taste?)*

CLARKE: Je n'ai pas vraiment faim. *(I'm not really hungry.)*

MARIE JEANNE: Pardon? *(Sorry?)*

CLARKE: Ce n'est pas la nourriture qui m'intéresse. *(It's not the food I'm interested in.)*

MARIE JEANNE turns away from CLARKE and goes back to her work.

Ne soyez pas timide. Vous vous êtes vendue à Louis pour une paire de gants et quelques épingles à cheveux. *(Don't be coy. You sold yourself to Louis for a pair of gloves and some hair-pins.)*

MARIE JEANNE: Je ne me suis pas vendue. Je suis là pour servir ma patrie. *(I didn't sell myself. I'm here to help my country.)*

CLARKE: Moi aussi, chérie. Et je préfère rester au chaud en le faisant. Deux par deux, comme le dit la Bible. *(Pause.)* Pourquoi êtes-vous toujours célibataire? *(Me too, dearie. And I'd rather keep warm while doing it. Two by two, like the Bible says… Why are you still single?)*

MARIE JEANNE: Vous cherchez une femme? *(You're looking for a wife?)*

CLARKE: Quelque chose comme ça. *(Something like that.)*

MARIE JEANNE: Avez-vous une maison? *(Do you have a house?)*

CLARKE: Bien sûr. *(Sure.)*

MARIE JEANNE: Et du bétail? Une poule au moins? *(And some livestock? A chicken at least?)*

He shakes his coin purse at her and clucks like a chicken.

Obtenez une poule, puis nous verrons. *(Get a chicken, then we'll see.)*

She goes back to tend the fire.

CLARKE: Je prendrai trois bols de soupe, deux avec du pain. *(I'll take three bowls of soup, two with bread.)*

MARIE JEANNE: *(Without missing a beat.)* Quatorze deniers. *(Fourteen pence.)*

CLARKE: Est-ce que vous lisez aussi bien que vous faites vos calculs? *(Is your reading as good as your arithmetic?)*

MARIE JEANNE: Oui. *(Yes.)*

CLARKE: Comment vous appelez-vous? *(What is your name?)*

MARIE JEANNE: Marie Jeanne.

CLARKE: Joseph Toussaint. Enchanté. *(Charmed.)*

JEAN-BAPTISTE: *(Calling from a distance.)* Toussaint!

CLARKE turns to see JEAN-BAPTISTE entering.

CLARKE: Jean-Baptiste! Viens rencontrer Marie Jeanne. Elle est une fille du roi. Pas mal, eh? Vive le roi Louis! *(Come meet Marie Jeanne. She's a daughter of the king. Not bad, right? Long live King Louis!)*

JEAN-BAPTISTE: *(Arriving in their midst.)* Louis n'est pas mon roi. *(Louis isn't my king.)*

CLARKE: She:kon, skennen'kó:wa ken? *(Hello, do you carry the Great Peace?)*

JEAN-BAPTISTE: Hen, Skennen'kó:wa. *(Yes, I carry the Great Peace.)*

He turns to greet MARIE JEANNE.

Bonjour, mademoiselle. She:kon. *(Hello.)*

MARIE JEANNE just stares at him.

CLARKE: Oh, regarde comment tu lui as fait peur, JB… Elle était très bavarde il y a une minute. *(Oh, look how much you scared her, JB… She was real chatty a minute ago.)*

JEAN-BAPTISTE: Wa'kerihwarónke sahtekionhne ahsewatenrononhne les Hollandais tatiteron. *(I heard you were down south making friends with the Dutch.)*

CLARKE: Toskeh. *(True.)* That was a shit investment. Little good it's done me.

JEAN-BAPTISTE: They've been good to the Kanien'kehá:ka *(Mohawk)*. And to all the Rotinonshonni *(Haudenosaunee)*.

CLARKE: Hen *(yes)*. Friendly, weren't they? It's a shame they're leaving.

JEAN-BAPTISTE: What, did your ugly face scare them away?

CLARKE: Ce n'est pas de ma faute, c'est les maudits anglais. Seiahre neh New Amsterdam? New York i:sken. Tanon ti British tehatikanereh akwekon neh onwentsa. C'est pour ça que Louis nous envoie ses soldats. *(It's not my fault, it's the fucking English. Remember New Amsterdam? Now it's New York. And those British bastards have their eyes on the whole territory. That's why Louis's sent us his soldiers.)*

JEAN-BAPTISTE: Et les chevaux. *(And the horses.)*

CLARKE: Et les fusils. *(And the guns.)*

MADAME SAVOIE enters.

MADAME SAVOIE: Monsieur.

CLARKE: Madame.

MADAME SAVOIE: Je ne vous connais pas. *(I don't know you.)*

CLARKE: Joseph Toussaint. Commerçant des biens européens et sauvages. *(Joseph Toussaint. Purveyor of European and Savage Goods.)*

MADAME SAVOIE: Marjolaine Savoie.

CLARKE: Savoie? Avez-vous un lien avec Capitaine Savoie? *(Any relation to Capitaine Savoie?)*

MADAME SAVOIE: My husband, yes.

CLARKE: Have there been any sightings of his ship?

MADAME SAVOIE: Not yet. *(To JEAN-BAPTISTE.)* You needn't trade here. Louis has provided for his men.

JEAN-BAPTISTE: They've got no snowshoes, nothing for the ice.

MADAME SAVOIE: It's only September.

JEAN-BAPTISTE: The snow will come before the next moon.

MADAME SAVOIE: The snow will come when God wills it so.

MARIE JEANNE: *(To JEAN-BAPTISTE.)* Vous avez un nom français, monsieur. *(You have a French name, monsieur.)*

CLARKE: Moi aussi. *(So do I.)*

MADAME SAVOIE: *(To MARIE JEANNE.)* Come. I have men for you to meet.

MARIE JEANNE: There are men here.

MADAME SAVOIE: Les commerçants *(traders)* do not make fit husbands.

MARIE JEANNE: What about the soldiers?

MADAME SAVOIE: They'll soon be out on campaign.

MARIE JEANNE: Is that a good idea? If there will be snow before the next moon?

MADAME SAVOIE: You will come with me, lest you disgrace yourself further.

MARIE JEANNE: I'm not disgracing myself, I'm working.

MADAME SAVOIE: Your work is to find a husband.

MARIE JEANNE: *(Pointing out JEAN-BAPTISTE.)* Maybe he could be my husband.

MADAME SAVOIE slaps MARIE JEANNE, shocking her. JEAN-BAPTISTE moves to intervene, but CLARKE discourages him.

MADAME SAVOIE: Talk like that is treason. For which you could easily hang. Would you like that? It's one way to avoid winter.

MARIE JEANNE: I'll get my cloak.

She exits.

CLARKE: *(To JEAN-BAPTISTE.)* I heard there was smallpox in your village. But your people are well? Sawatsireh? *(Your family?)* There are medicines, you know.

JEAN-BAPTISTE: We have our own medicine. Sahonrá:ien ken? *(Do you have rifles?)*

CLARKE: Kanien tewakaton hontsió:ni, eso. *(I need flint. Lots of it.)*

JEAN-BAPTISTE: Wakiwharakateh, nektsi iah ne ne kanien. *(I have furs. No flint.)*

CLARKE: The Kanien'kehá:ka *(Mohawk)* are going to need new allies.

JEAN-BAPTISTE: The Kanien'kehá:ka *(Mohawk)* have the Rotinonshonni *(Haudenosaunee).*

MADAME SAVOIE returns. JEAN-BAPTISTE takes his leave of CLARKE but stops near the back of the outdoor kitchen as MARIE JEANNE returns.

CLARKE: Rassembler les gamines et les putains, et les envoyer ici pour se marier. Pas mal comme idée… *(Gather up the whores and street kids, ship them over and marry them off. Not the worst idea…)*

MADAME SAVOIE: Ce sont des femmes honnêtes. *(They are honest women.)*

CLARKE: *(Laughing.)* Ce n'est pas la place pour des femmes honnêtes. Que leur avez-vous promis? Un mari aimant et une vie paisible? *(This isn't the place for honest women. What did you promise them? A loving husband and a peaceful life?)*

MADAME SAVOIE: They came willingly.

CLARKE: I've seen them in the fields, the farmers' wives. Pulling the plow because they had to eat the horse. It's going to be a long winter.

MADAME SAVOIE: Winter is always long.

CLARKE: Some extra provisions would serve you well.

MADAME SAVOIE: I am well provided for.

CLARKE: Sure, but who'll provide for the girls?

CLARKE looks to MARIE JEANNE. MADAME SAVOIE turns and sees MARIE JEANNE and JEAN-BAPTISTE, whose eyes are locked on each other. CLARKE tips his hat to MADAME SAVOIE.

Madame.

CLARKE exits.

MADAME SAVOIE: *(To JEAN-BAPTISTE.)* Tosah. *(Stop that.)* *(To MARIE JEANNE.)* Restez près de moi. *(Stay close to me.)*

The women exit hurriedly. JEAN-BAPTISTE watches them go.

Scene 4

Later that same day. Evening. The chapel at l'Hôtel-Dieu. KATERI emerges from behind the altar, carrying a beaver pelt. She stands very still, listening. She walks around, exploring the space. She turns and is startled by the sight of Jesus on the cross. She takes a long look. She hears MADAME SAVOIE and MARIE JEANNE approaching, and hides behind the altar.

MADAME SAVOIE: *(Offstage.)* Ce sont des barbares cruels. *(They're cruel barbarians.)*

MARIE JEANNE: Il m'a salué cordialement. *(He greeted me politely.)*

MADAME SAVOIE: Ils sont manipulateurs. Si vous étiez capturée, vous souhaiteriez la mort. *(They're manipulative. If you were captured, you would be wishing for death.)*

MARIE JEANNE: Que font-ils aux captifs? *(What do they do to captives?)*

MADAME SAVOIE: À genoux. Demandez à Dieu qu'il vous protège. *(On your knees. Ask God to protect you.)*

MARIE JEANNE kneels. MADAME SAVOIE leaves. MARIE JEANNE prays, eyes closed.

MARIE JEANNE: JE VOUS SALUE, MARIE
JE VOUS SALUE, MARIE PLEINE DE GRÂCE
LE SEIGNEUR EST AVEC VOUS
(Hail Mary
Hail Mary, full of grace
The Lord is with thee)

As MARIE JEANNE continues her prayer, KATERI quietly comes out from behind the altar. She studies MARIE JEANNE, then kneels on the ground close by, imitating her exactly.

VOUS ÊTES BÉNIE ENTRE TOUTES LES FEMMES
ET JÉSUS, LE FRUIT DE VOS ENTRAILLES
EST BÉNI, SAINTE MARIE MÈRE DE DIEU
PRIEZ POUR NOUS, MARIE
PAUVRES PÉCHEURS
MAINTENANT ET À L'HEURE DE NOTRE MORT
(Blessed art thou among women
And Jesus, the fruit of thy womb
Is blessed, Holy Mary, Mother of God
Pray for us, Mary
Poor sinners
Now and in the hour of our death)

Amen.

KATERI: Amen.

MARIE JEANNE screams and scrambles to her feet. She heads for the exit.

She:kon. *(Hello.)*

MARIE JEANNE stops. She turns back towards KATERI. KATERI raises one hand in a small, unthreatening wave.

Kateri ióntiats. *(My name is Kateri.)* Ka-te-ri.

MARIE JEANNE: Ka-te-ri…?

KATERI: Hen, Ok ní:se'? *(Yes, and yours?)*

She gestures towards MARIE JEANNE, then to herself.

Akwá:wen Kateri, í:se ken…? *(Mine Kateri, yours…?)*

MARIE JEANNE: Moi?

KATERI: Hen, í:se. *(Yes, you.)*

MARIE JEANNE: Je m'appelle Marie Jeanne. Marie Jeanne. *(My name is Marie Jeanne. Marie Jeanne.)*

KATERI: Wully Jen.

MARIE JEANNE: Oui! *(Yes!)*

KATERI: *(She points to herself.)* Un. *(Indicating both of them.)* Deux.

MARIE JEANNE: *(Repeating the gesture.)* Oui, nous sommes deux. Deux filles. *(Yes, there are two of us. Two girls.)*

KATERI: Filles? *(Girls?)*

MARIE JEANNE: Oui, nous sommes des filles. Pas des garçons, mais des filles. *(Yes, we're girls. Not boys, but girls.)*

KATERI: Nahoten ne ne fille? *(What is "fille"?)*

MARIE JEANNE: *(She points to herself.)* Fille. *(Girl.) (She mimes breasts.)* Femme. *(Woman.) (Lost for an example, she points to Jesus.)* Homme. *(Man.)*

KATERI: Tho, tho. Naho:ten ronwa:iats? *(Yes, yes. What is his name?)*

MARIE JEANNE: Sur la croix? C'est notre Seigneur Jésus Christ. Jésus. *(On the cross? That's our Lord Jesus Christ. Jesus.)*

KATERI: Jay-zoo?

MARIE JEANNE: Oui, c'est ça! Jésus. *(Yes, that's it! Jesus.)*

KATERI: Iesos. Tho, tho. *(Jesus. That's right.)*

She heads up toward the altar to take a closer look. MARIE JEANNE calls out to her.

MARIE JEANNE: Non, pas en haut là. On reste içi. On ne monte jamais à l'autel. *(No, not up there. We stay here. We never go up on the altar.)*

KATERI notices the lace on MARIE JEANNE's dress and reaches for her sleeve.

KATERI: Oh ni:iot enshi:ron...ki:ken? *(How do you say... what's this?)*

Touching the lace on MARIE JEANNE's dress.

Ki:ken, ki:ken? *(This, what's this?)*

MARIE JEANNE: La dentelle? *(The lace?)*

KATERI: Dundel.

MARIE JEANNE: Oui. Dentelle. *(Yes. Lace.)*

KATERI: Tho, tho. *(That's it.)*

KATERI presents the beaver pelt to MARIE JEANNE.

MARIE JEANNE: C'est magnifique... Si beau, si doux. *(It's wonderful... So beautiful, so soft.)*

KATERI gets up and puts the pelt around MARIE JEANNE's shoulders.

KATERI: Wully Jen akohsera'kéhkha akià:tawi. *(Marie Jeanne's winter coat.)*

She points to MARIE JEANNE's sleeve.

Kateri, dentelle. *(Kateri, lace.)*

MARIE JEANNE: Un échange? La dentelle contre la fourrure? *(A trade? The lace for the fur?)*

KATERI: Tho, tho. *(Yes, that's right.)*

She takes out a knife.

Enwa:ton ken…? *(May I…?)*

MARIE JEANNE: Et pourquoi pas? *(And why not?)*

MARIE JEANNE takes the knife, and roughly cuts the lace from her dress, leaving the sleeves ragged. She gives the lace to KATERI, and KATERI gives her the fur.

KATERI: Nià:wen. Orihwí:io. Wesatshennónni ken? *(Thank you. That's good business. Are you happy?)*

MARIE JEANNE: Je ne comprends pas… Wésutte…? *(I don't understand… Wésutte…?)*

KATERI: Wesatshennónni. *(Happy.)*

She makes a happy face.

Kateri. Wakatshennónni. *(Kateri. I'm happy.)*

She gestures to MARIE JEANNE.

Í:se. Wully Jen. Wesatshennónni ken? *(You. Marie Jeanne. Are you happy?)*

MARIE JEANNE: Oui. Oui, merci. *(Yes. Yes, thank you.)*

KATERI: Way-see?

MARIE JEANNE: Je te remercie. Merci. *(I thank you. Thank you.)*

KATERI: *(Understanding.)* Wayr-see. Nià:wen. *(Thank you.)*

Niawenhkó:wa. *(Thank you very much.)*

MARIE JEANNE: Ni-a-w-i-en. *(Thank you; mispronounced.)*

JEAN-BAPTISTE enters and sees the girls.

JEAN-BAPTISTE: Kateri. Teiotonhontsió:hon ahsatá:séhte. *(You're supposed to be hiding.)*

KATERI: Satkato, raktsi:ah. Watkatà:ton. *(Look, big brother. My first trade.)*

JEAN-BAPTISTE: Ka'nontásaweh? *(Where did you get this?)*

MARIE JEANNE: Bonjour. *(Hello.)*

He takes in MARIE JEANNE's ragged sleeves.

JEAN-BAPTISTE: *(To KATERI.)* Did you do that?

KATERI: We made a trade.

JEAN-BAPTISTE: You traded our finest pelt for some useless cloth?

KATERI: It's not useless.

JEAN-BAPTISTE: We don't need it. *(To MARIE JEANNE.)* Je suis désolé, ma soeur a ruiné votre robe. *(I'm sorry my sister ruined your dress.)*

MARIE JEANNE: C'est votre soeur? *(She's your sister?)*

JEAN-BAPTISTE: Oui. *(Yes.)*

MARIE JEANNE: Je croyais qu'elle était votre femme. *(I thought she was your wife.)*

JEAN-BAPTISTE: *(To MARIE JEANNE.)* Non. *(No.)* *(To KATERI.)* A teaching; the French are obsessed with marriage.

MARIE JEANNE: She can have the lace. I don't need it. But take the fur back, please. It must be very valuable.

JEAN-BAPTISTE: It is.

MARIE JEANNE: I can't keep it.

JEAN-BAPTISTE: A trade is a trade.

KATERI: Let's take her back to our kanata *(village).*

JEAN-BAPTISTE: Í:iah thaón:ton. *(We can't do that.)*

KATERI: Iakoianeh *(Clan Mother)* says we need more people, to help with the harvest. Satkato ne ietsianà:ke. *(Let's see her hands.)*

(*To MARIE JEANNE.*) Sahtsóhare. *(Hands.)*

She grabs MARIE JEANNE's hands. MARIE JEANNE, misunderstanding, kisses KATERI's hand in thanks.

MARIE JEANNE: Oui, merci. Niá:wen. *(Yes, thank you. Thank you.)*

L'ESPACE (Space)

KATERI: Hánio. *(Come on.)*

KATERI takes MARIE JEANNE's hand and leads her up towards the altar.

JEAN-BAPTISTE: Iah, iah Kateri. *(No, Kateri, don't.)*

MARIE JEANNE: Qu'est ce qui se passe? *(What's happening?)*

JEAN-BAPTISTE: Ne vous inquiétez pas, vous restez ici. *(Don't worry, you're staying here.)*

MARIE JEANNE: J'aimerais voir à l'extérieur du fort. *(I would like to see outside the fort.)*

KATERI: *(To JEAN-BAPTISTE.)* Onkiátsi ne' kí:ken. *(She's my friend.)*

MARIE JEANNE: J'AIMERAIS VOIR CE QU'IL Y A
DE L'AUTRE BORD DE CES MURS
(I'd like to see what's out there
on the other side of these walls)

JEAN-BAPTISTE: Les soldats vont vous arrêter. *(The soldiers will stop you.)*

MARIE JEANNE: J'AIMERAIS ME PROMENER LIBREMENT AVEC VOUS
RASSEMBLONS-NOUS AUTOUR D'UN BEAU FEU DOUX
ENSEMBLE MANGEONS, PARLONS ET PARTAGEONS
(I'd like to roam freely with you
Let's gather 'round a nice warm fire
Together let's eat, talk, share)

Again, KATERI takes MARIE JEANNE's hand and pulls her up toward the altar.

JEAN-BAPTISTE: Kateri.

KATERI: Tetkehtà:kwa, raktsi:ah. *(I trust her, brother.)*

JEAN-BAPTISTE: *(To MARIE JEANNE.)* Il y a un petit passage là, derrière l'autel. Ça vous amènera dehors, vers la rivière. Rencontrez-nous là demain, au coucher du soleil. Hánio, Kateri. *(There's a small door up there behind the altar. It will take you down a passage to the river. Meet us there tomorrow at sundown. Come on, Kateri.)*

KATERI: O:nen, Wully Jen. *(Goodbye, Marie Jeanne; mispronounced.)*

KATERI and JEAN-BAPTISTE exit.

MARIE JEANNE: J'AIMERAIS L'ESPACE POUR GRANDIR ET DEVENIR QUI JE SUIS
J'AIMERAIS LE POUVOIR DE CHOISIR UN HOMME QUI
PARTAGE AVEC GÉNÉROSITÉ, PRENDS SOIN DE MOI
SANS VOULOIR ME LIMITER
(I'd like the space to grow up and become who I really am
I'd like the power to choose a man who
Shares generously, takes care of me
Without wanting to limit me)

LES FILLES begin to enter. They watch MARIE JEANNE as they sing, gathering behind her.

MARIE JEANNE & FILLES:

JE VEUX DE L'ESPACE
JE VEUX DE L'AIR PUR
UN CIEL QUI S'OUVRE À MOI
CE PAYS S'ÉTEND MILLE FOIS
(I want space
I want pure air
A sky that opens itself to me
This land stretches out a thousand times)

(Overlapping.) JE VEUX DE L'ESPACE
JE VEUX DE L'AIR PUR
UN CIEL QUI S'OUVRE À MOI
CE PAYS S'ÉTEND MILLE FOIS
(I want space
I want pure air
A sky that opens itself to me
This land stretches out a thousand times)

CHORUS ECHO: JE VEUX UN JARDIN
JE VEUX DES ENFANTS
RESSENTIR LA JOIE
CE PAYS S'ÉTEND MILLE FOIS
(I want a garden
I want children
To feel joy
This land stretches out a thousand times)

CHORUS LEAD: JE VEUX UN NAVIRE
JE VEUX ÊTRE SOLDAT
JE VEUX MA PROPRE CHANSON
CE PAYS S'ÉTEND MILLE FOIS
(I want a sailing ship
I want to be a soldier
I want my own song
This land stretches out a thousand times)

CHORUS ECHO: JE VEUX UNE MAISON
JE VEUX POUVOIR LIRE
UN BON GARÇON
CE PAYS S'ÉTEND MILLE FOIS
(I want a house
I want to be able to read
A nice boy
This land stretches out a thousand times)

The land opens up and we are taken back to France, in a vision of the women's lives before this journey.

MOTHER: NEXT YEAR WE'LL COME TO JOIN YOU
YOUR FATHER, BROTHERS AND I
SO PROUD OF OUR ONLY DAUGHTER, THAT I
MAY BREAK DOWN AND CRY
SAYING GOODBYE

FILLE: HOW WILL YOU FIND ME THERE?
THEY SAY THE WORLD IS BIGGER THERE
THAN HERE

ALL MOTHERS: SEND US A MAP

ALL FILLES: IF I DON'T LEAVE HERE NOW
SICKNESS WILL TAKE ME FIRST, I FEAR

ALL: EVERYTHING WET AND COLD AND LEAKING
THIS DIRTY CITY SEWER REEKING

INSTRUMENTAL. LES FILLES are at a dance in France, celebrating the women who are heading off to the New World, having one last goodbye with their family and friends.

LES FILLES ready themselves for their travels. MARIE JEANNE and LISE ANNE are in their room, packing for their journey.

MARIE JEANNE: LISE ANNE, DON'T BE AFRAID
I AM HERE FOR YOU
WE ARE A PART OF IT ALL
TOGETHER LIKE QUEENS
SISTER, YOU AND I
WE'RE OFF TO FIND THE NEW WORLD

ALL: WE WON'T BE AFRAID OF THE ROAD AHEAD
WE ARE A PART OF IT ALL
LIVING THE LIVES THAT OUR FAMILIES DREAMT
WE'RE OFF TO FIND THE NEW WORLD

INSTRUMENTAL. LES FILLES are on the ship travelling to the New World. In the middle of a storm, they are tossed from side to side, holding onto one another, trying to stay on their feet. As the ship slows its rocking, SAILORS appear and separate LISE ANNE from MARIE JEANNE.

Separated from the other FILLES, LISE ANNE is seduced by an officer on the ship.

LISE ANNE: HE WAS KIND AND POLITE, A TRUE GENTLEMAN
HE SWEPT ME OFF OF MY FEET
STRANGERS WOULD PASS SAYING
"MY GOOD MAN"
BUT THEY'RE WRONG, HE'S NOT A GOOD MAN

HE GRABS MY HAND, HE PULLS MY HAIR
HE DRAGS ME DOWN A LONG DARK HALLWAY
I THINK I'LL DIE
IF I DON'T LEAVE HERE NOW THIS IS THE LAST TIME I SWEAR
LIE ON THE GROUND, HE'S BARELY MOVING
I SNEAK AWAY TO FIND HIM LOOMING OVER ME

ALL: WE WON'T BE AFRAID OF THE ROAD AHEAD
WE ARE A PART OF IT ALL
LIVING THE LIVES THAT OUR FAMILIES DREAMT
WE'RE OFF TO FIND THE NEW WORLD
WE WON'T BE AFRAID OF THE ROAD AHEAD
WE ARE A PART OF IT ALL
LIVING THE LIVES THAT OUR FAMILIES DREAMT
WE'RE OFF TO FIND THE NEW WORLD

INSTRUMENTAL. LES FILLES are standing at the edge of the ship saying goodbye to their families. Behind them, MARIE JEANNE and LISE ANNE are hugging, saying goodbye through their tears.

As each woman steps away from the edge of the ship, LISE ANNE says one last goodbye to MARIE JEANNE. LISE ANNE leaves, then jumps off the ship. MARIE JEANNE is alone.

In MADAME SAVOIE's quarters at the Hotel-Dieu, CLARKE enters with a stack of provisions and puts it on her desk. MADAME SAVOIE hands him some money.

CLARKE: Marjolaine…

MADAME SAVOIE: You'll receive the rest when my husband returns.

CLARKE: You know Jean-Baptiste would have given you a better price.

MADAME SAVOIE: I don't trust him.

CLARKE: Why don't you trust les Iroquois?

MADAME SAVOIE: I don't trust any of them. They're all the same.

CLARKE: No, they're not.

MADAME SAVOIE: True, some have become good Catholics, some have not.

CLARKE: And that's the only distinction that matters.

MADAME SAVOIE: Yes.

CLARKE: I admire your faith. But honestly I don't see how it helps you here. *(Pause.)* What if your husband's ship doesn't come in? They left La Rochelle seven months ago.

MADAME SAVOIE: I can count, thank-you.

CLARKE: We could make an alternate arrangement.

MADAME SAVOIE: You don't strike me as the type to settle down and milk a cow.

CLARKE: That's what the wife is for. *(Pause.)* She'll be one of the lucky ones. I've already got land, a house…

MADAME SAVOIE: You've built a house?

CLARKE: Even got some chickens.

Scene 5

The following night, as MARIE JEANNE arrives at KATERI and JEAN-BAPTISTE's camp by the river.

MARIE JEANNE: JE VEUX DE L'ESPACE
JE VEUX DE L'AIR PUR
UN CIEL QUI S'OUVRE À MOI
CE PAYS S'ÉTEND MILLE FOIS
(I want space
I want pure air
A sky that opens itself to me
This land stretches out a thousand times)

JEAN-BAPTISTE and KATERI are at their camp; MARIE JEANNE is with them. They are all gathered round the fire.

KATERI: *(To JEAN-BAPTISTE.)* Shehrori tsi takerihonnienni ne takataton tanon taiakwataren ne kiohroksaka. *(Tell her you're teaching me how to trade and talk to white people.)*

MARIE JEANNE: Je ne sais pas ce que ça veut dire. *(I don't know what that means.)*

JEAN-BAPTISTE: Je lui enseigne à faire la traite des fourrures avec Kiohrohsaka – avec les hommes blancs – et à parler un peu le français. *(I'm teaching her to trade furs with the white people, and some French.)*

MARIE JEANNE: Qu'est-ce que ton frère t'a déjà appris? Kateri, français? *(What has your brother already taught you? Kateri, French?)*

KATERI: Un, deux, trois. *(One, two, three.)*

JEAN-BAPTISTE: Ioianére, konkén:'a. *(Very good, sister.)*

KATERI: Fourrures, fort… filles. *(Furs, fort… girls.)* *(To JEAN-BAPTISTE.)* Sheri'wanontons aionkerihónnien owenasonah. *(Ask her to teach me some new words.)*

JEAN-BAPTISTE: Elle veut que tu lui apprennes à dire quelque chose. *(She wants you to teach her how to say something.)*

MARIE JEANNE: Il nous faut du bois. *(We need more wood.)*

KATERI: Ee noo fah doo bwa. Nahoten ne kenton? *(What does that mean?)*

JEAN-BAPTISTE: It means we need more enkientakoha *(firewood).*

He gets up.

KATERI: Iah, sakien. *(No, sit.)* I'll do it.

JEAN-BAPTISTE: Iah tetehshientéri ne kahakon. *(You don't know these woods.)*

KATERI: I won't go far, je promets. *(I promise.)*

She heads off, but JEAN-BAPTISTE mimics a bird call, stopping her in her tracks. Exasperated, she turns back.

Raktsi:ah, enke'nikonrará:ke'. *(Brother, I'll listen to my mind.)*

He does it again.

Iaseh takakia'táhton. *(I won't get lost.)*

He does it again. She answers back with a slightly modified version of the call.

JEAN-BAPTISTE: Ioianere. Wahs, o:nen enwáton ensahténti. *(Good. Now you may go.)*

KATERI goes off to collect firewood.

MARIE JEANNE: You and your sister are close.

JEAN-BAPTISTE: She's not going to be a trader.

MARIE JEANNE: Because she'll be married?

JEAN-BAPTISTE: When she's older, she's going to be Iakoianeh – our Clan Mother. She'll be a leader.

MARIE JEANNE: Your women are allowed to lead?

JEAN-BAPTISTE: They make sure our Hoyaneh – Chief – is hearing everyone's voice, and making good decisions.

MARIE JEANNE: That's very… different.

JEAN-BAPTISTE: I don't think we could have it any other way. Kateri sees people for who they are; she has it in her.

MARIE JEANNE: How did you get the name Jean-Baptiste?

JEAN-BAPTISTE: I don't look like a Jean-Baptiste?

MARIE JEANNE: Not at all.

JEAN-BAPTISTE: My father was French. He lived among the Kanien'kehá:ka until I was five. Then he had to go back.

MARIE JEANNE: He lived among the Gani…gaga…?

JEAN-BAPTISTE: The Kanien'kehá:ka.

MARIE JEANNE: Kanien'kehá:ka.

JEAN-BAPTISTE: Yeah. And he married my mother.

MARIE JEANNE: I didn't know that the French married… you… people. I didn't know that people did that, or were able to do that.

JEAN-BAPTISTE: We are all just people. *(Pause.)* Why did you come here?

MARIE JEANNE: I'm a *fille du roi.*

JEAN-BAPTISTE: Royalty? Oh no, now we're really in trouble.

MARIE JEANNE: Not really. But sent by the King, to populate the New World.

JEAN-BAPTISTE: It's already populated.

MARIE JEANNE: I see that now, yes.

JEAN-BAPTISTE: Where are your people?

MARIE JEANNE: It's just me.

JEAN-BAPTISTE: You came here alone?

MARIE JEANNE: No. My sister Lise Anne... She was with me on the boat. But she didn't survive the journey.

JEAN-BAPTISTE: I'm sorry.

MARIE JEANNE: You could drink the dirty water, or give yourself to the sailors. Lise Anne refused to do either. So she jumped. But she wasn't a coward. She was... made of something else. Uncompromising. True to herself. Kateri reminds me of her.

JEAN-BAPTISTE: So you came here to get married.

MARIE JEANNE: I did.

JEAN-BAPTISTE: But you're not married.

MARIE JEANNE: Not yet.

JEAN-BAPTISTE: Who's the lucky man?

BEYOND THE WALLS

MARIE JEANNE: Will more of your people come to this village?

JEAN-BAPTISTE: This is just our camp. Our kanata – the village – is down the river, south then west.

MARIE JEANNE: I'd like to see it someday.

JEAN-BAPTISTE: No way. That would set off the French.

MARIE JEANNE: It's happened before though; like you said, with your father.

JEAN-BAPTISTE: My father was a simple trader, I don't think anyone even realized he was gone. But a *fille du roi,* they'd fight to protect your honour. I know they would.

MARIE JEANNE: IF YOU'D ASKED ME TODAY
HOW THIS NIGHT WOULD END
I'D NEVER HAVE THOUGHT OF THIS
I'M GLAD THAT YOU'RE HERE

JEAN-BAPTISTE: I'M GLAD THAT YOU STAYED

BOTH: SOON YOU'LL HAVE TO GO

MARIE JEANNE: WE SAT UNDER THE STARS

JEAN-BAPTISTE: YOU SAW BEYOND THE WALLS

BOTH: NOW TAKE A GOOD LOOK
FOR ALL THAT YOU SEE
YOU'LL HAVE TO SAY
GOODBYE

KATERI enters with a bundle of sticks and pinecones she's gathered for the fire. She drops them loudly, breaking the charged silence.

KATERI: Oh niiohtonhákie? *(How is it going?)*

JEAN-BAPTISTE and MARIE JEANNE avoid her gaze, and each other.

Raktsi:ah *(big brother)*, you're so bad at conversation. Even though trade takes a lot of talking, you're really not good at it, are you? I hope you didn't offend her… She's all red.

She adds wood and stokes the fire, unaware of the tension between JEAN-BAPTISTE and MARIE JEANNE.

MARIE JEANNE: THEY SAID BEYOND THE WALLS
IT WOULD BE UNSAFE AND WILD
THEY SAID THE PEOPLE HERE
WOULDN'T BE SO KIND AND MILD
THEY HAVE BEEN HERE
FAR MUCH LONGER THAN WE REMEMBER
I'D BE FINE IF I STAYED HERE THROUGH THE NIGHT
I KNOW THAT HE'D TAKE CARE
WOULDN'T LEAVE, I KNOW HE'D FIGHT
IT'S BEEN TOO LONG
SINCE I'VE HAD SOMEONE TO BE THERE

BOTH: CE QUE TU RESSENS, VAS-Y, RACONTE
EMPARE-TOI DE CE MOMENT, À CHAQUE SECONDE
C'EST LE MOMENT D'ÊTRE BRAVE,
IL FAUT QUE TU T'ÉLANCES
SI NOUS HÉSITONS,
NOUS GASPILLONS CETTE CHANCE
(This thing you're feeling, go on, say it
Seize this moment, every second
It's time to be brave
You have to throw yourself into it
If we hesitate
We'll waste this chance)

MARIE JEANNE and JEAN-BAPTISTE are now outside the gates of Ville-Marie.

MARIE JEANNE: Thank you. I could have found my own way, but thank you.

JEAN-BAPTISTE: And how would you have done that?

MARIE JEANNE: Follow the river.

JEAN-BAPTISTE: You should stay within the fort. Always. Goodbye, mademoiselle…?

MARIE JEANNE: Lespérance. Marie Jeanne Lespérance.

JEAN-BAPTISTE: L'espérance? *(Hope?)* That's a good name. And a nice idea.

MARIE JEANNE: IF YOU'D ASKED ME TODAY
HOW THIS NIGHT WOULD END
I'D NEVER HAVE THOUGHT OF THIS
I'M GLAD THAT YOU'RE HERE

JEAN-BAPTISTE: I'M GLAD THAT YOU STAYED

BOTH: NOW YOU HAVE TO GO
WE SAT UNDER THE STARS

MARIE JEANNE: I SAW BEYOND THE WALLS

BOTH: NOW TAKE A GOOD LOOK
FOR ALL THAT YOU SEE
WE'LL HAVE TO SAY
GOODBYE

MARIE JEANNE leaves. JEAN-BAPTISTE watches her go, then exits.

In the chapel, MARIE JEANNE appears behind the altar. MADAME SAVOIE is standing near the altar, waiting for her.

MADAME SAVOIE: Just as I thought. Sneaking around, and desecrating His sacred space with your deceit!

MARIE JEANNE: I wasn't doing anything bad.

MADAME SAVOIE: Never in all my years have I met such a stupid, ungrateful girl.

MARIE JEANNE: I just wanted to see beyond the walls of the fort.

MADAME SAVOIE: Who did you go to meet?

MARIE JEANNE: No one.

MADAME SAVOIE: Tell me his name.

MARIE JEANNE: I was visiting a farmer. Those are the men I'm supposed to meet.

MADAME SAVOIE: Until you are married, you have no business spending time alone with any men. But of course, you are used to spending time with them. You did so on the ship, and back in France too, so why would that change here?

MARIE JEANNE: Madame, I am good. I promise you that, here before God.

MADAME SAVOIE: Then pray to God to save you, because as hard as I try, you refuse to let me help you.

MARIE JEANNE: You don't care about me, or any of the girls.

MADAME SAVOIE: Winter is days away. And once it comes, that's it, we are at its mercy.

MARIE JEANNE: We have winter in France.

MADAME SAVOIE: You don't know what winter is. You have no idea. I've survived twenty winters because I married. And when my husband died, I married again. And when he died, I married again. I have seen what happens to girls who ignore good advice.

MARIE JEANNE: You're saying this to scare me.

MADAME SAVOIE: I'm saying it because it's the truth.

MARIE JEANNE: No decent man will want me, Madame.

MADAME SAVOIE: There are some men who see beyond such things. Leave it to me. Everything will be fine.

MARIE JEANNE: Oui, Madame. *(Yes, Madame.)*

MADAME SAVOIE: Good girl.

They exit together down the aisle.

Scene 6

SICKNESS

CHORUS: OOOOH

KATERI and JEAN-BAPTISTE are at the riverside, packing up their canoe to head back to their village.

KATERI: Don't you want to tell her that we're leaving?

JEAN-BAPTISTE: As soon as we're packed up to go, we'll let her know.

KATERI: I can sneak back in and tell her.

JEAN-BAPTISTE: No, you're not allowed to be seen in the fort. You put us at risk, Kateri.

KATERI: Wully Jen *(Marie Jeanne; mispronounced)* won't tell anyone.

JEAN-BAPTISTE: *(Hearing something.)* Kats, aknakon testa'n. *(Get behind me.)*

(Calling out.) Toussaint.

CLARKE appears from the trees, and JEAN-BAPTISTE signals for KATERI to go to the canoe.

CLARKE: She:kon. *(Hello.)*

JEAN-BAPTISTE: Skennen'kó:wa ken? *(Do you carry the Great Peace?)*

CLARKE: Hen, skennen'kó:wa. *(Yes, I carry the Great Peace.)* I saw some Oneida braves cross the kanién'tara *(river)* a couple days ago. Didn't think much of it, but then the Seneca and the Cayuga came to the fort, and now…

JEAN-BAPTISTE: And now the Onondaga are meeting with the Kanekien – hen, wakaterientareh *(the French – yes, I know).*

CLARKE: Were the Kanien'kehá:ka *(Mohawk)* not invited?

JEAN-BAPTISTE: Hakats *(come on),* Kateri. *(To CLARKE.)* See you in the spring.

CLARKE: All your brother nations in the Rotinonshonni *(Haudenosaunee)* are siding with the Kanekien *(French).*

JEAN-BAPTISTE: Eh kati tho. *(So be it.)*

CLARKE: ONWATON ONKOIENAWASEH
ENTA'ONK AKATERIENTARA'NE
ONHKA TEHSESWANONHA
ENIETSIIATAKEHA NE SAKIOKWA
NE SAKIOKWA
(I can help you
But I need to know
where you stand
This could save your people
Your people)

JEAN-BAPTISTE: IAH SHE ONKA ENTAONK
TAIENKI:IENAWASEH
Add KATERI: IAH SHE ONKA ENTAONK
TAIENKI:IENAWASEH
(We don't need saving)
(We don't need saving)

CLARKE: Kanekien ratiteronton atsiaktonkeh tanon British ne neh enkie nonkwá:ti. *(There are French forts all along the river, and now you're surrounded by the British to the south.)*

JEAN-BAPTISTE: The French would be interested in knowing there's a Britishman in their colony.

CLARKE: How long have you known?

JEAN-BAPTISTE: You may have the French fooled, but you move like a soldier.

CLARKE: Let me write the Duke of York and tell him we've got the Kanien'kehá:ka *(Mohawk)* onside.

JEAN-BAPTISTE: IAH SEH NI'I ROIANEH TEKEN *(I'm not a War Chief)*

CLARKE: EH TSHEHRORI KI NEH ROIANEH *(Then tell your Chief)*

JEAN-BAPTISTE & KATERI:
IAH SE EHTEIOT NE KARIWASONAH KAKWATAKWEN
(That's not the way decisions are made)

CLARKE:
ONWATON ONKOIENAWASEH
ENTA'ONK AKATERIENTARA'NE
ONHKA TEHSESWANONHA
ENIETSIIATAKEHA NE SAKIOKWA
NE SAKIOKWA
(I can help you
But I need to know
where you stand
This could save your people
Your people)

If I were you, I'd try to speed things along.

JEAN-BAPTISTE: No one would wage war in winter.

CLARKE: You'd be surprised what we're prepared to do. I'm on my way to marry a Frenchwoman. And that is fucking awful. Remember Marie Jeanne? Sure, she's a *fille du roi*… but we know they're all whores.

CLARKE exits.

KATERI: YOU ARE UPSET
WHAT DID HE SAY?

JEAN-BAPTISTE: HE PLANS TO MARRY MARIE JEANNE
BY END OF DAY

KATERI: WE CAN TELL HER WHAT WE KNOW
THERE'S STILL TIME BEFORE THE SNOW

In the French fort at Ville-Marie, MADAME SAVOIE is waiting on the steps of the chapel.

MADAME SAVOIE: À CHAQUE ANNÉE QU'IMPORTE NOS EFFORTS
IL Y A TOUJOURS UNE FILLE DU ROI QUI MEURT
CHAQUE ANNÉE JE FAIS TOUT CE QUE JE PEUX
MAIS MALGRÉ ÇA, ELLE SE RETROUVE AUX CIEUX
(Every year, no matter what we do
There's always a girl who dies
Every year, I do the best I can
And yet, she finds herself up in heaven)

FILLE 1: WHO CAN HEAR THE WORDS I'M SAYING?
WHO CAN UNDERSTAND?

Add FILLE 2: WE CAN FEEL THE SEASONS CHANGING
WE CAN FEEL THE SICKNESS SETTING IN

ALL FILLES: WARM NIGHTS TURNING COLD
WE THE YOUNG GROW OLD
WHO WILL TAKE THIS VOW?
WHO WILL FIND ME NOW?

MARIE JEANNE enters, wearing her cloak and the beaver pelt. She joins MADAME SAVOIE on the steps of the chapel.

MARIE JEANNE: It's so cold, Madame. Much colder than yesterday.

MADAME SAVOIE: Stop whining. I have good news.

MADAME SAVOIE holds out a document.

MARIE JEANNE: What's this?

MADAME SAVOIE: Your marriage contract.

MARIE JEANNE: Who am I marrying?

MADAME SAVOIE: Sign it.

As MARIE JEANNE signs the contract, LES FILLES transform into SOLDIERS.

MARIE JEANNE, MADAME SAVOIE & FILLES:

WHO CAN HEAR THE WORDS I'M SAYING?
WHO CAN UNDERSTAND?
WE CAN FEEL THE SEASONS CHANGING
WE CAN FEEL THE SICKNESS SETTING IN

JEAN-BAPTISTE and KATERI enter the fort. They run to MARIE JEANNE, but MADAME SAVOIE steps between them.

MADAME SAVOIE: *(To JEAN-BAPTISTE, re: KATERI.)* What is she doing in the fort?

JEAN-BAPTISTE: Marie Jeanne, I need to talk to you.

He rushes towards MARIE JEANNE. As MADAME SAVOIE moves to protect MARIE JEANNE, she and JEAN-BAPTISTE collide and MADAME SAVOIE is knocked to the ground. She calls out desperately to the nearby SOLDIERS.

MADAME SAVOIE: Soldiers, restrain le sauvage *(the savage)!*

The SOLDIERS lay hands on JEAN-BAPTISTE.

(To KATERI.) You, come with me.

MARIE JEANNE: Wait, where are you taking her?

MADAME SAVOIE: She cannot be in the fort unless she has accepted God into her heart.

MADAME SAVOIE grabs KATERI and pulls her into the chapel.

JEAN-BAPTISTE: Let her go!

The SOLDIERS hit and subdue JEAN-BAPTISTE, binding his hands. The PRIEST enters.

KATERI: Ketsanis, raktsi:ah. *(I'm scared, big brother.)* Will it hurt?

JEAN-BAPTISTE: No. The water will be cold, but it won't hurt. Everything will be fine.

KATERI's baptism begins.

ALL:
COLD TO THE BONE, I'M NEEDING HOME
SWEET HOME
COLD TO THE BONE, I'M NEEDING HOME
SWEET HOME

KATERI:
IF I ASK WHY I HAVE TO LIE
IF YOU STAND BY, I'LL HAVE TO LIE

CLARKE arrives on the steps of the chapel. MADAME SAVOIE goes to meet him.

MADAME SAVOIE: Finally. Sign here.

MARIE JEANNE: But he's not a farmer.

MADAME SAVOIE: He will take care of you.

MARIE JEANNE: How?

MADAME SAVOIE: All the other girls have married and left the Hôtel-Dieu.

CLARKE rolls up the certificate and tucks it into his coat.

CLARKE: Pleasure doing business with you, Madame.

MADAME SAVOIE: *(To MARIE JEANNE.)* At least with him, you stand a chance.

ALL: COLD TO THE BONE, I'M NEEDING HOME
SWEET HOME
COLD TO THE BONE, I'M NEEDING HOME
SWEET HOME

MADAME SAVOIE & CLARKE:
(*Overlapping.*) WHO CAN HEAR THE WORDS I'M SAYING?
WHO CAN UNDERSTAND?
WE CAN FEEL THE SEASONS CHANGING
WE CAN FEEL THE SICKNESS SETTING IN

KATERI: (*Overlapping.*) TOAH ENTAONK NONKEREH TSI ENKANONWENTEH
TOAH KENTENSTANEH, ENTAONK ENKANONWENTEH
(If I ask why I have to lie
If you stand by, I'll have to lie)

MARIE JEANNE: (*Overlapping.*) SOIRÉES DOUCES ÉCOULÉES
FROID PROFOND, FILLE ÂGÉE
QUI ME PRENDRA LA MAIN?
QUI SUIVERA MON CHEMIN?
(Warm nights slipped through my fingers
Now this deepest cold, girl gone old
Who will take my hand?
Who will follow where this leads?)

CHORUS: (*Overlapping.*) WARM NIGHTS TURNING COLD
WE THE YOUNG GROW OLD
WHO WILL TAKE THIS VOW?
WHO WILL FIND ME NOW?

JEAN-BAPTISTE: (*Overlapping.*) IOTOREH,
TEWAKATONHONTSION:NI AONSAKATONTI
IOTOREH, TEWAKATONHONTSION:NI
AONSAKATONTI
(Cold to the bone, I'm needing home sweet home
Cold to the bone, I'm needing home sweet home)

CHORUS: OOOOH

MARIE JEANNE looks to CLARKE, who extends his hand. She hesitates, then looks to JEAN-BAPTISTE.

MARIE JEANNE: I'm sorry.
JE VEUX DE L'ESPACE
JE VEUX DE L'AIR PUR
(I want space
I want pure air)

CLARKE's impatience grows. The PRIEST dunks KATERI's head in the font of water.

UN CIEL QUI S'OUVRE À MOI
(A sky that opens itself to me)

MARIE JEANNE extends her hand to CLARKE, but before she makes contact –

CE PAYS S'ÉTEND MILLE FOIS
(This land stretches out a thousand times)

KATERI emerges from the water and gasps for air. MARIE JEANNE and CLARKE exit as the snow begins to fall.

Scene 7

Winter. January – March 1666. Evening.

WINTER (Instrumental)

SOLDIERS grab JEAN-BAPTISTE and take him to a dark cell.

KATERI shows signs of illness. She is escorted by MADAME SAVOIE to the hospital where she crawls into bed. MADAME SAVOIE prays at her bedside.

A small, drafty house outside Ville-Marie. MARIE JEANNE enters, struggling with an armful of wood and kindling. She is stiff with cold, and struggles to build a fire. Finally, she gets a candle, and lights it from the fire, as MADAME SAVOIE strikes a match. MARIE JEANNE places the candle on the table.

MADAME SAVOIE lights a candle. She sits at KATERI's bedside, pulls out a Bible and begins reading. KATERI recoils under the blankets.

CLARKE enters, stamping snow from his boots, startling MARIE JEANNE. She gets up and pulls out a chair. He takes off his hat, scarf and coat, dropping it all on the floor.

MADAME SAVOIE gets up and pulls up a stool to sit on.

CLARKE goes to the fire. MARIE JEANNE picks up his coat off the floor and hangs it on the chair. She finds a letter in his coat pocket.

MADAME SAVOIE holds the book out to KATERI and teaches her the words. KATERI slowly emerges from the blankets, interested.

MARIE JEANNE opens and reads the letter she found in CLARKE's coat.

KATERI takes the book from MADAME SAVOIE, first examining its shape and binding, then looking through it, turning the pages.

CLARKE catches MARIE JEANNE reading his letter, rushes over and snatches it from her hands. He hits her, hard.

MADAME SAVOIE takes KATERI's hand and begins to pray. KATERI looks around, awkward.

CLARKE gets ink, a quill, and parchment, which he sets on the table in front of MARIE JEANNE. He puts her to work copying the letter.

MADAME SAVOIE pulls out her rosary and gives it to KATERI, showing her all the different beads, then begins to pray once again.

CLARKE takes the letter MARIE JEANNE has been copying. He reads it over, folds it, and puts it in his pocket. He approaches her and leans close, whispering in her ear. She recoils. He exits. After a moment, she follows dutifully.

COLD ISN'T PERMANENT

JEAN-BAPTISTE: I SLEEP ALONE IN THIS CORNER
WITH NO LIGHT, ONLY DARKNESS AROUND ME
THE AIR IS MUCH COLDER
I AM WEAK, WHAT WILL HAPPEN TO ME?
AND THOUGH I DON'T HAVE MUCH HEAT
A RAGING FIRE AT MY FEET

WE SING WAY YAH
TO WARM UP OUR LIPS
SINGING WAY YAH
TO WARM INSIDE OF ME
WE SING WAY YAH
COLD ISN'T PERMANENT
WAY YAH
WELCOMING SIGNS OF SPRING

SOLDIERS enter and remove JEAN-BAPTISTE's shackles. They take him to the hospital, where he is met by MADAME SAVOIE.

Kateri. Où est-elle? *(Kateri. Where is she?)*

MADAME SAVOIE: Merci de l'avoir amenée ici. Il se peut que le diable s'empare d'elle, mais Dieu merci; nous l'avons baptisé avant qu'il soit trop tard. Vous êtes libre de partir. *(Thank you for bringing her to us. The devil may still be alive in her, but thank God; we baptized her in time. You are free to go.)*

JEAN-BAPTISTE: Maintenant? *(Now?)*

MADAME SAVOIE: Après vos adieux. Elle est gravement malade. Ne vous inquiétez pas; quand elle meurt, elle ira au paradis vivre une vie éternelle. *(After you say goodbye. She's very sick. Don't worry; when she dies, she'll go to heaven and live an eternal life.)*

MADAME SAVOIE and SOLDIERS exit. JEAN-BAPTISTE enters the hospital room. He goes to KATERI's bedside and grabs her hand.

JEAN-BAPTISTE: YOU HAVE THE SOUL OF A FIGHTER
YOU HAVE OUR ANCESTORS ALL RIGHT INSIDE YOU
AS STUBBORN AS FATHER WAS
SMART AND KIND JUST LIKE OUR MOTHER WAS
AND WHILE THEY MAY NOT BE HERE
WE WILL CALL TO THEIR EAR

WE SING WAY YAH
TO WARM UP OUR LIPS
SINGING WAY YAH
TO WARM INSIDE OF ME
WE SING WAY YAH
COLD ISN'T PERMANENT
WAY YAH
WELCOMING SIGNS OF SPRING

JEAN-BAPTISTE: Sata'karí:te ken? *(Are you healthy?)*

KATERI: Yah, yah sata'karí:te. *(No I am not healthy.)*
HERE THE AIR IS MUCH COLDER
THAN I REMEMBER BEFORE
THE WINTER IS LONGER
AND THE CHILL LINGERS ON

JEAN-BAPTISTE puts his forehead down on her hand.

I SING WAY YAH
DON'T WORRY, BROTHER
WAY YAH
THIS WILL MOVE ON
WITH THIS WAY YAH
I WILL FEEL BETTER
WAY YAH
REMEMBERING THIS WINTER'S GONE
Je me sens mieux maintenant. *(I'm feeling better now.)*

JEAN-BAPTISTE: That was perfect! Who taught you that?

KATERI: The woman in the black robe. She came every day and spoke to me in her language. She told me the story of Atsi'tsiaká:ion *(Sky Woman)* but with different names. She got a lot of things wrong though; we should really help her get the story right. *(Pause.)* Oh nahò:ten kénton "baptisé"? *(What does it mean, "baptized"?)*

JEAN-BAPTISTE: It's one of their ceremonies. You need to be baptized to come into the fort.

KATERI: Am I still Bear Clan?

JEAN-BAPTISTE: Yes. Always.

JEAN-BAPTISTE & KATERI:

WE SING WAY YAH
TO WARM UP OUR LIPS
SINGING WAY YAH
TO WARM INSIDE OF ME
SINGING WAY YAH
COLD ISN'T PERMANENT
WAY YAH
WELCOMING SIGNS OF SPRING

KATERI: WAY YAH HEY YAH WAY YO

KATERI & JEAN-BAPTISTE:

WAY YAH HEY YO, WAY YAH HEY YO
WE NA MA HEY YAH HEY YO
WAY YAH HEY YO, WAY YAH HEY YO

CHORUS: *(Offstage.)* WAY YAH HEY YAH WAY YO
WAY YAH HEY YO, WAY YAH HEY YO
WE NA MA HEY YAH HEY YO
WAY YAH HEY YO, WAY YAH HEY YO

WAY YAH HEY YAH WAY YO
WAY YAH HEY YO, WAY YAH HEY YO
WE NA MA HEY YAH HEY YO
WAY YAH HEY YO, WAY YAH HEY YO

She shows him the crucifix on her rosary.

KATERI: Look what she gave me.

JEAN-BAPTISTE: You don't have to keep that.

KATERI: But I want to. Look how it shines in the light.

JEAN-BAPTISTE: Leave it, Kateri. I'm taking you home.

JEAN-BAPTISTE removes her rosary and leaves it hanging on the bedpost. He picks her up, and they leave the hospital.

Scene 8

March, 1666. Snow and wind. A single candle burns, nearing the end of its wick. MARIE JEANNE prays on her knees, rosary in hand.

QUI ME SAUVERA

MARIE JEANNE: JE VOUS SALUE, MARIE
JE VOUS SALUE, MARIE PLEINE DE GRÂCE
LE SEIGNEUR EST AVEC VOUS
VOUS ÊTES BÉNIE ENTRE TOUTES LES FEMMES
ET JÉSUS, LE FRUIT DE VOS ENTRAILLES
EST BÉNI, SAINTE MARIE MÈRE DE DIEU…
(Hail Mary
Hail Mary, full of grace
The Lord is with thee
Blessed art thou among women
And Jesus, the fruit of thy womb
Is blessed, Holy Mary, Mother of God…)

She stands up.

IL N'Y A PERSONNE LÀ, PERSONNE ME RÉPONDRA
Y-A-T'IL QUELQU'UN LÀ, QUELQU'UN QUI M'AIDERA?
J'SUIS SÉPARÉE D'CELUI À QUI JE PENSE TOUJOURS
ON M'A VOLÉ LA CHANCE DE VIVRE UN VRAI AMOUR
ET MAINTENANT JE SUIS SEULE ET QUE DOIS-JE FAIRE?
JE SUIS TOUTE SEULE PIÉGÉE DANS L'INFERNAL HIVER
IL N'Y A PERSONNE LÀ, PERSONNE ME RÉPONDRA
IL N'Y A QUE MOI, C'EST MOI-MÊME, QUI ME SAUVERA

(There's no one there, no one will answer me
Is there someone there, someone who can help me?
I'm separated from the one I think of still
My chance for true love was stolen from me
And now I'm alone, and what must I do?
I'm all alone trapped in this infernal winter
There is no one there, no one will answer me
There's only me, it's me alone, who will save me)

She puts her rosary in her apron pocket and gets her cloak.

PRIEZ POUR MOI, MARIE
PAUVRES PÉCHEURS
MAINTENANT ET À L'HEURE DE NOTRE MORT
(Pray for me, Mary
Poor sinners
Now and in the hour of our death)

MARIE JEANNE puts on her cloak and turns to go, but she is interrupted by CLARKE returning home.

CLARKE: You going on a trip?

MARIE JEANNE: Vous avez mangé toute la nourriture. *(You ate all the food.)*

CLARKE: I was hungry. *(Pause.)* How far do you think you'll get?

MARIE JEANNE: Vous avez promis de prendre soin de moi pendant tout l'hiver. Mais il n'y a plus rien à manger, et il y a encore de la neige au sol. *(You promised to provide for us over the winter. But we have nothing left to eat, and there's still snow on the ground.)*

CLARKE: This colony is a fucking disaster.

MARIE JEANNE: C'est pour ça que tout le monde rationne! *(That's why everyone is rationing!)*

CLARKE: You're such a child. I have money.

MARIE JEANNE: L'argent ne peut pas acheter la nourriture qui n'existe pas. J'ai fait tout ce que vous m'avez demandé – j'ai même espionné mes gens. *(Money can't buy food that doesn't exist. I've done everything you asked – even helped you spy on my own people.)*

CLARKE: You've copied a few letters, don't flatter yourself.

MARIE JEANNE: Parce que vous m'aviez dit que j'aurais tout ce dont j'ai de besoin. Mais ce n'est pas le cas. *(Because you said I would be taken care of. But that hasn't happened.)*

CLARKE: You know I can't let you go.

MARIE JEANNE: Vous n'avez pas le choix. *(You don't have a choice.)*

CLARKE: You won't survive out there.

MARIE JEANNE: Mes chances sont meilleures toute seule qu'avec toi. *(My chances are better out there on my own, than here with you.)*

SICKNESS (Reprise)

CHORUS: OOOOOH

MARIE JEANNE heads for the door, but CLARKE grabs a knife and launches himself at her. She fights back, knocking the knife out of his hand. He pushes her to the ground and kicks her in the stomach. She grabs his leg and bites him. He drags her across the floor, but she gets up, grabs the knife and stabs him in the stomach.

CHORUS: OOOOOH

CLARKE falls to the ground. MARIE JEANNE puts down the knife, grabs her cloak, and leaves the house.

In the chapel of the Hotel-Dieu, MADAME SAVOIE prays. In Ville-Marie, outside the chapel, JEAN-BAPTISTE and KATERI run into MARIE JEANNE.

CHORUS: OOOOOH

MARIE JEANNE: Jean-Baptiste! Kateri… Is she all right?

JEAN-BAPTISTE: She's sick.

KATERI: I'm getting better.

MARIE JEANNE: *(To JEAN-BAPTISTE.)* And you? Sata'karí:te ken? *(Are you healthy?)*

JEAN-BAPTISTE: I'm fine. I'm taking her back to our kanata *(village).*

MADAME SAVOIE comes out of the chapel and observes them, unseen.

MARIE JEANNE: I need your help. I think I killed him.

JEAN-BAPTISTE: What? Who?

MARIE JEANNE: Toussaint – or whoever the hell he is. They'll hang me.

JEAN-BAPTISTE: Come with us.

MARIE JEANNE, JEAN-BAPTISTE and KATERI leave together. From the steps of the chapel, MADAME SAVOIE watches them go.

MADAME SAVOIE addresses the French military leaders.

MADAME SAVOIE: Il a tué un commerçant français et s'est enfuit avec une de nos filles du roi. Les Iroquois refusent de s'allier avec nous, et maintenant ils assassinent des colons à l'intérieur de nos remparts. Si vous n'intervenez pas, je vais écrire à sa Majesté le Roi, et je lui dirai que vous permettez le massacre sur cette sainte terre. *(He has killed a French trader and taken hostage one of our filles du roi. The Iroquois have refused to align with us and are killing colonists within our own walls. If you do not intervene, I will write to the King and tell him you are allowing slaughter on his Holy Ground.)*

À CHAQUE ANNÉE, QU'IMPORTE NOS EFFORTS
LE MONDE ICI RAVAGE MON ESPOIR
MAIS CETTE ANNÉE, JE FERAI TOUT C'QUE JE PEUX
MÊME SI CETTE FILLE SE TROUVERA AUX CIEUX
(Every year, no matter what we do
These insufferable savages destroy our hopes
But this year, I'll do everything I can
Even if it means that girl finds herself in Heaven)

ÉCOUTEZ, J'SUIS ÉCOEURÉE
J'PEUX PLUS, J'EN AI ASSEZ
FILLE PERDUE, SAUVAGES QUI TUENT
CHRIST, MAUDIT, CE FORT EST UN CALVAIRE
(Listen, I'm fed up
I can't do this anymore, I've had enough
A girl lost to murdering savages
Cursed Christ, this place is a mess)

FROID MORDANT
ET FEUX D'ENFER, ENFER
MOI LA SEULE QUI SAIT QUOI FAIRE
MAIS QUOI FAIRE?
(This biting cold
And these hellish fires, hell itself
I'm the only one who knows what to do
But what to do?)

MADAME SAVOIE exits. LES FILLES enter slowly from the other side.

FILLE: *(Solo.)* WAY YAH HEY YAH WAY YO
WAY YAH HEY YO, WAY YAH HEY YO

Add 2nd FILLE: WE NA MA HEY YAH HEY YO
WAY YAH HEY YO, WAY YAH HEY YO

The women gather at centre, swaying slowly as they sing.

WAY YAH HEY YAH WAY YO
WAY YAH HEY YO, WAY YAH HEY YO
WE NA MA HEY YAH HEY YO
WAY YAH HEY YO, WAY YAH HEY YO

The women separate and slowly begin circling around one FILLE. In the centre of the circle, this FILLE removes her skirt and shawl, transforming into the CLAN MOTHER. Another FILLE hands her a drum, and CLAN MOTHER begins drumming. LES FILLES continue circling CLAN MOTHER.

WAY YAH HEY YAH WAY YO
WAY YAH HEY YO, WAY YAH HEY YO
WE NA MA HEY YAH HEY YO
WAY YAH HEY YO, WAY YAH HEY YO

Another FILLE separates from the circle. She transforms into a WOMAN OF THE LONGHOUSE and joins CLAN MOTHER. LES FILLES continue circling. CLAN MOTHER begins drumming double-time.

WAY YAH HEY YAH WAY YO
WAY YAH HEY YO, WAY YAH HEY YO
WE NA MA HEY YAH HEY YO
WAY YAH HEY YO, WAY YAH HEY YO

(Add harmonies.) WAY YAH HEY YAH WAY YO
WAY YAH HEY YO, WAY YAH HEY YO
WE NA MA HEY YAH HEY YO
WAY YAH HEY YO, WAY YAH HEY YO

The remaining FILLES begin setting up the Longhouse, as the singing continues.

Scene 9

Spring. May 1666. Dawn. At the Kanien'kehá:ka village, the sun is rising and peeking through the Longhouse. The CLAN MOTHER is drumming and singing; a WOMAN OF THE LONGHOUSE sings with her, dancing close by. It is a warm spring day.

KATERI and MARIE JEANNE enter with baskets of food; corn, beans, and squash. They go over to CLAN MOTHER, and KATERI joins in the singing.

WAY YAH HEY YAH WAY YO
WAY YAH HEY YO, WAY YAH HEY YO
WE NA MA HEY YAH HEY YO
WAY YAH HEY YO, WAY YAH HEY YO

KATERI and MARIE JEANNE set down the food baskets and sit together with a WOMAN OF THE LONGHOUSE. KATERI invites MARIE JEANNE to sing along, and she does, gradually learning the melody. The WOMAN OF THE LONGHOUSE takes MARIE JEANNE to sit over by the fire.

WAY YAH HEY YAH WAY YO
WAY YAH HEY YO, WAY YAH HEY YO
WE NA MA HEY YAH HEY YO
WAY YAH HEY YO, WAY YAH HEY YO

CLAN MOTHER looks over at KATERI, who is sitting alone.

SKÉN:NEN KOWA (Great Peace)

(Overlapping.) WAY YAH HEY YAH WAY YO
WAY YAH HEY YO, WAY YAH HEY YO
WE NA MA HEY YAH HEY YO
WAY YAH HEY YO, WAY YAH HEY YO

CLAN MOTHER: YOU HAVE YOUR ISTA'S *(mother's)* EYES
SHINING DARK AND DEEPLY WISE
SHE PASSED THESE WAMPUM STRANDS TO YOU

BOYS BECOME MEN EVERYDAY
YOU WILL CHOOSE OUR HOYANEH *(Chief)*
YOUR GOAL WILL BE TO FILL THIS ROLE

YOU'LL WATCH THEM GROW
TEACH THEM ALL YOU KNOW
RAISE THEM TO BE HONEST, BRAVE AND TRUE
IAKOIANEH *(Clan Mother)*, THIS WILL BE ALL UP TO YOU, TO YOU

EAST IS LOST WITHOUT THE WEST,
KEEPING BALANCE NEVER RESTS
WHEN WE HAVE ALL WE'LL EVER NEED

WE ARE FEWER THAN BEFORE
SICKNESS REACHES TO OUR CORE
IN TIME OUR PEOPLE WILL RISE.

YOU'LL WATCH THEM GROW
TEACH THEM ALL YOU KNOW
RAISE THEM TO BE HONEST, BRAVE AND TRUE
IAKOIANEH, THIS WILL BE ALL UP TO YOU, TO YOU

The WOMAN OF THE LONGHOUSE stands up. She begins to sing with CLAN MOTHER. She invites MARIE JEANNE to stand and sing, which she does. The ANCESTORS enter, adding their voices.

KARIHWAKWENIENHTSHERA
GAYANEREKOWA
SHARENHOWANE
SKARONHESEKO:WA
TSIOKTERAKENTKO:WA
(Respect the Great Law,
the tree branching out,
the ever-growing tree)

WE'LL WATCH YOU GROW
BECOMING WHO WE KNOW
YOU'LL BE THE LEADER WE KNOW YOU CAN BE
IAKOIANEH YOU WILL FIND A WAY TO SEE

KA'SHASTENSERA KONTIHAWE NE IOTIIANE:SHON
SKÉN:NEN KOWA
(With the Women's Nomination Belt,
carry the Great Peace)

As the song ends, KATERI brings MARIE JEANNE over to the food baskets.

KATERI: Marie Jeanne, nahoten kiken? *(Marie Jeanne, what's this?)*

MARIE JEANNE: Onaste. *(Corn; mispronounced)*

KATERI: Non, comme on dit *en*fant, *en*semble. O'nenste. *(No, like child, together. Corn.)*

MARIE JEANNE: O'nenste. *(Corn)*

KATERI: Et ceux-ci? *(And these here?)*

MARIE JEANNE: O'sahè:ta. *(Beans.)*

KATERI: Satsiron. *(Say it again.)*

MARIE JEANNE: O'sahèta. *(Beans.)*

KATERI: Pas mal. *(Not bad.)*

She shows MARIE JEANNE a piece of squash.

Onon'onhsera. *(Squash.)*

MARIE JEANNE: Onon'onhsera. *(Squash.)*

KATERI: Ioianére *(good)*. Comment dit-on onon'onhsera en français? *(How do you say onon'onhsera in French?)*

JEAN-BAPTISTE enters the Longhouse.

MARIE JEANNE: Je n'ai jamais vu ça avant d'arriver ici. *(I'd never seen it before coming here.)*

KATERI: Vous n'avez pas ahsen ni kontate'kén:à? *(You don't have the Three Sisters?)*

MARIE JEANNE: Ahsen kiken…? *(Three what…?)*

KATERI gestures as she speaks, explaining.

KATERI: Ahsen ni kontate'kén:à. Elles grandissent ensemble. O'nenste est la plus grande, comme ça. O'saheta grimpe la tige. Et en bas, les feuilles du Onon'onhsera s'étalent et fournissent l'ombre, ce qui fait que le sol reste humide. Les twa – trrrrois – ensemble, comme une famille. *(The Three Sisters. They grow together. Corn is the tallest, like this. The beans climb up the stalk. And down here, the leaves of the squash spread out and give shade, so the soil stays damp. The three all together, like a family.)*

JEAN-BAPTISTE joins the women, kneeling next to KATERI.

JEAN-BAPTISTE: Oh niiohtonhákie? Sata'karí:te ken? *(How is it going? Are you healthy?)*

KATERI: Hén, yoyanerátye. *(Yes, it's going good.)*

JEAN-BAPTISTE: *(To MARIE JEANNE.)* Sateweniesta kanien:kéha? *(You're learning Mohawk?)*

MARIE JEANNE: If I'm going to stay in the kanata *(village)*, I need to learn how to speak with your people.

JEAN-BAPTISTE: You plan to stay with us?

MARIE JEANNE: I would like to.

KATERI: I would like that too.

JEAN-BAPTISTE: You can't. I'm sorry.

WE COULD BE

KATERI: Where will she go?

JEAN-BAPTISTE: I want you to be safe, but you can't stay here… you put us at risk, threaten our entire community.

MARIE JEANNE: No one saw us leave the fort. If they think I made it past the gates, they'll just assume I'm dead.

KATERI: Tho tho *(that's right)*, there's no way she could survive out here on her own.

MARIE JEANNE: I'll work hard, I won't be a burden.

KATERI: Iakoianeh *(Clan Mother)* will decide.

KATERI goes over to talk with CLAN MOTHER.

MARIE JEANNE:
THIS PLACE, HERE, THIS IS ALL THAT I HAVE NOW
EVERYTHING ELSE HAS BEEN TAKEN
DROWNED IN THE SEA, OR UP IN HEAVEN

THIS HAND, YOU, YOU ARE ALL THAT I HAVE NOW
YOU ARE THE REASON I'M LIVING
DRAWING THIS BREATH TO SAY
PLEASE LET ME STAY

JEAN-BAPTISTE:
I CAN'T THINK OF JUST MYSELF
I CAN'T THINK OF YOU ALONE
LOOK AROUND, IMAGINE WHAT COULD BE
EVERYONE YOU SEE, THEY ALL DEPEND ON ME

IF I THINK OF JUST MYSELF
I WOULD THINK OF YOU ALONE
LOOK AT ME AND TELL ME WHAT YOU SEE
IF ONLY IT WAS ME, MY ANSWER WOULD BE

MARIE JEANNE: I KNOW, I HEAR YOUR HEART, HOW IT'S BEATING
FROM THE FIRST TIME THAT I SAW YOU

BOTH: I KNEW WE'D NEVER SEE WHAT WE COULD BE

A drum begins to beat, fast and loud. MARIE JEANNE coughs. KATERI and the CLAN MOTHER enter the Longhouse, warning JEAN-BAPTISTE.

TOSAH ENSATERENAIEN
(Don't Pray to Your God)

MARIE JEANNE: L'air est épais. *(The air is thick.)*

KATERI: Ioienkwarote, raktsi:ah. *(It's smoke, brother.)*

JEAN-BAPTISTE: Oksah, satrehnionni tanon onake satitah. *(Hurry, pack your things, and get in the canoe.)*

KATERI: Je l'apporte à l'autre rive. Si le feu saute par dessus la rivière, on restera sur l'eau à bord du canot. *(I'll take her across the water. If the fire jumps the river, we'll stay on the water in the canoe.)*

There is a large fire burning in the village. There is panic and screaming; everyone is trying to escape. The Longhouse begins to crumble; one of the walls crashes down.

MARIE JEANNE: Qu'est-ce qui se passe? *(What's happening?)*

JEAN-BAPTISTE: Allez vous-en! Peu importe ce que vous voyez, ne revenez pas. *(Get out! Whatever you see, don't come back across.)*

KATERI and MARIE JEANNE escape the Longhouse. SOLDIERS ransack and attack; JEAN-BAPTISTE fights them off then runs into the burning woods, the SOLDIERS following.

In a canoe, KATERI and MARIE JEANNE paddle across the choppy water. They land on the opposite shore and watch the flames rip across the landscape.

KATERI: Ontaonk thoientoweh, ahtsaktonkeh rones rononkwe, sekens keneh rononkwe? *(We have to go back, there are people on the shore. Do you see them?)*

MARIE JEANNE: Non, je ne peux rien voir. Trop de fumée. *(No, I can't see anything. Too much smoke.)*

KATERI: Tho, tsi non weh neh awenkeh tanon iohnontahere. *(Right there, next to where the cliff meets the water.)*

MARIE JEANNE sees the people KATERI is pointing at. She takes out her rosary, grabs KATERI's hand, and drops to her knees on the shore.

MARIE JEANNE: JE VOUS SALUE, MARIE
J'VOUS SALUE, MARIE PLEINE DE GRÂCE
(Hail Mary
Hail Mary, full of grace)

KATERI: Ils ont l'uniforme des soldats français. *(They're wearing uniforms. It's French soldiers.)*

MARIE JEANNE: JE VOUS EN PRIE, MARIE
PROTÈGE-LE DE CES FLAMMES VORACES
(I beg you, Mary
Protect him from these voracious flames)

KATERI: La madame m'a dit que les français sont ici pour nous sauver. *(But the madame said the French were here to save us.)*

MARIE JEANNE: PARDONNE C'QUE J'AI FAIT
PARDONNE-MOI SI C'EST D'MA FAUTE
(Forgive what I've done
Forgive me if it's all my fault)

KATERI: C'est ton peuple qui nous fait ça? *(It's your people who are doing this to us?)*

MARIE JEANNE: JE N'AVAIS PAS PRÉVU…
J'N'AURAIS JAMAIS VOULU CE MALHEUR
*(I didn't expect…
I never wanted this tragedy)*

KATERI rips her hand out of MARIE JEANNE's. She grabs the rosary and throws it.

KATERI: TOSAH, TOSAH ENSATERENAIEN
ISEH TSHESEWAWEN:NI:IO
EHNAHAIEREH NE IONKWAHONSTA
EHNAHAIEREH NE IONKWAHONSTA
(Stop that! Don't pray to your God. Your God who has brought so much devastation to this land.)

(Overlapping.) TOSAH, TOSAH
ENSATERENAIEN
ISEH TSHESEWAWEN:NI:IO
EHNAHAIEREH NE IONKWAHONSTA
EHNAHAIEREH NE IONKWAHONSTA
(Stop that! Don't pray to your God. Your God who has brought so much devastation to this land.)

MARIE JEANNE: *(Overlapping.)* JE M'INQUIÈTE POUR TON FRÈRE
JE M'INQUIÈTE POUR CE QU'IL VA FAIRE TOUT SEUL…
CROIS-MOI JE L'AIME AUTANT QUE TOI
CROIS-MOI J'N'AI JAMAIS VOULU CELA
*(I'm worried about your brother
I'm worried about what he'll do all alone…
Believe me, I love him as much as you do
Believe me, I never wanted this)*

KATERI: AUPARAVANT NOUS NE TOMBIONS PAS MALADE
AUPARAVANT N'SOUFFRAIT PAS MA PEUPLADE
J'N'AVAIS PAS ENTERRÉ LE CHER CORPS DE MA MÈRE
J'N'AVAIS PAS VU TON PEUPLE DÉSHONORER NOTRE TERRE...
(Before, we didn't get sick
Before, my people didn't suffer
I hadn't buried my dear mother's body
I hadn't seen your people dishonour our land...)

AKWEWEKON NE KEHNORONKWA
TOAHENHONNIHEIEH SOK SONHAK
TANON ENTAON TENKONSHEN NEKSI IA
TESEWEIENTEH NEH AHSONEKEH
(Everyone I love could soon be gone
And then I'll only have you
And I'll have to take care of you
Because you don't even know how to live)

CHORUS: *(Offstage.)* WE WON'T BE AFRAID OF THE ROAD AHEAD
WE ARE A PART OF IT ALL
LIVING THE LIVES THAT OUR FAMILIES DREAMT
WE'RE OFF TO FIND THE NEW WORLD

The girls stand in silence, and watch the village burn.

Scene 10

The next day, back at the village. KATERI and MARIE JEANNE stand on the shore. KATERI does the bird call for JEAN-BAPTISTE. Silence. She does it again. Silence. She breaks down. MARIE JEANNE approaches slowly, placing her hand on KATERI's shoulder. MARIE JEANNE attempts the call. Silence. She tries again. From a distance, JEAN-BAPTISTE returns the call.

FINALE

KATERI and MARIE JEANNE run towards the sound. JEAN-BAPTISTE emerges from the woods, black with soot and struggling to walk.

KATERI: Raktsi:ah! *(Big brother!)*

She hugs him. He winces.

You're hurt.

JEAN-BAPTISTE: Just my arm.

KATERI: What about the others?

JEAN-BAPTISTE: Most made it out in time and took refuge up the mountain.

MARIE JEANNE: The soldiers, are they still a threat?

JEAN-BAPTISTE: They burned all our villages from east to west, then took off in the night. We'll start the journey west to the Oneida, as soon as we join the others.

He and KATERI start to exit.

MARIE JEANNE: I assume I'm not welcome.

JEAN-BAPTISTE turns to look at her.

JEAN-BAPTISTE: We will all go together.

She goes to join them, then stops.

MARIE JEANNE: *(To JEAN-BAPTISTE.)* What will happen to this village?

KATERI: We will rebuild.

KATERI offers her hand to MARIE JEANNE. She takes it, and they exit together.

Scene 11

FINALE (Continued)

Summer 1666. On the shore by Ville-Marie. MADAME SAVOIE greets a new ship arriving with more FILLES DU ROI.

FILLES: LA GLOIRE, LA FRANCE ET LE BON DIEU
C'EST POUR LUI QUE NOUS SOMMES TOUTES ICI
ET POUR LOUIS LE ROI SOLEIL
QUI M'A CHOISI
(For glory, for France and our merciful Lord
We're all here for Him
And for Louis the Sun King
Who has chosen me)

TRAVERSER A FAILLI ME TUER
MALGRÉ LES TEMPÊTES, LA MALADIE
JE SUIS ICI, NOUS SOMMES ICI
LES FILLES DU ROI
(The crossing nearly killed me
But in spite of all the storms and sickness
I'm here, we're all here
The daughters of the King)

KATERI, JEAN-BAPTISTE, and MARIE JEANNE enter. From the shore, they see the ship and the NEW WOMEN arriving.

(Overlapping.) UNE DERNIÈRE FOIS J'DIS AU REVOIR
J'M'APPRÊTE À RENCONTRER MA GLOIRE
J'RETOURNERAI JAMAIS À PARIS
L'AVENIR SE TROUVE ICI
(One final goodbye
Getting ready to go meet my glory
I'll never again go back to Paris
The future is here before me)

J'AI MA CASSETTE: UNE PAIRE DE BAS,
UNE COIFFE, UN BONNET, UN MOUCHOIR
DES GANTS, DES ÉPINGLES, DES AIGUILLES
DU FIL ET DES CISEAUX
(I've got my trousseau: a pair of socks,
A comb, a bonnet, a handkerchief
Gloves, some pins, some needles
Some thread and scissors)

KATERI: *(Overlapping.)* ARE THOSE GIRLS THE SAME AS ME?
BROTHER, LET'S GO DOWN AND SEE

JEAN-BAPTISTE: *(Overlapping.)* STAY BY MY SIDE, WE'LL WATCH FROM HERE
YOU FOOLISH GIRLS, SO MUCH TO FEAR

MARIE JEANNE & LISE ANNE:
(Overlapping.) J'AIMERAIS VOIR CE QU'IL Y A DE L'AUTRE BORD DE CES MURS
J'AIMERAIS ME PROMENER LIBREMENT AVEC VOUS
RASSEMBLONS-NOUS AUTOUR D'UN BEAU FEU DOUX
ENSEMBLE MANGEONS, PARLONS ET PARTAGEONS
(I'd like to see what's out there
on the other side of these walls
I'd like to roam freely with you
Let's gather 'round a nice warm fire
Together let's eat, talk, share)

FILLES: *(Overlapping.)* JE VEUX DE L'ESPACE
JE VEUX DE L'AIR PUR
UN CIEL QUI S'OUVRE À MOI
CE PAYS S'ÉTEND MILLE FOIS
(I want space
I want pure air
A sky that opens itself to me
This land stretches out a thousand times)

MADAME SAVOIE & PRIEST:
(Overlapping.) HABITANTS, REGARDEZ LES BELLES FILLES DU ROI
LES BIJOUX DE NOTRE PATRIE
FILLETTES, CHOISISSEZ-VOUS UN BON MARI
DONNEZ-VOUS AU NOM DE LOUIS
(Habitants, look; the pretty daughters of the King
The jewels of our homeland
Girls, choose yourselves a good husband
Give yourselves in the name of Louis)

FILLES: *(New overlap begins.)* LES VOILÀ, LES CÉLIBATAIRES
UNE CENTAINE D'HOMMES, QUE DOIS-JE FAIRE?
MON MARIAGE EST IMMINENT
MAIS QUI CHOISIR, COMMENT?
(Look, there they are, the bachelors
A hundred men, what should I do?
My marriage, it's imminent
But who to choose, and how?)

C'EST POUR LOUIS, LA FRANCE, ET LE SEIGNEUR
LOUIS, LA FRANCE, ET LE SEIGNEUR
LOUIS, LA FRANCE, ET LE SEIGNEUR
JE FERAI MON DEVOIR
(I'm doing this for Louis, for France, and the Good Lord
For Louis, France, and the Good Lord
For Louis, France, and the Good Lord
I will do my duty)

JEAN-BAPTISTE: *(Overlapping.)* LES FILLES DU ROI, WHY ARE YOU HERE?
PLEASE JUST GO HOME, OR DISAPPEAR

KATERI: *(Overlapping.)* LES FILLES DU ROI, CAN YOU HEAR ME?
WHAT IS IT LIKE ACROSS THE SEA?

MARIE JEANNE & LISE ANNE:
(Overlapping.) J'AIMERAIS L'ESPACE POUR GRANDIR ET DEVENIR QUI JE SUIS
J'AIMERAIS LE POUVOIR DE CHOISIR UN HOMME QUI
PARTAGE AVEC GÉNÉROSITÉ, PRENDS SOIN DE MOI
SANS VOULOIR ME LIMITER
(I'd like the space to grow and become who I am
I'd like the power to choose a man who
Shares generously, takes care of me
Without wanting to limit me)

FILLES: *(Overlapping.)* JE VEUX DE L'ESPACE
JE VEUX DE L'AIR PUR
UN CIEL QUI S'OUVRE À MOI
CE PAYS S'ÉTEND MILLE FOIS
(I want space
I want pure air
A sky that opens itself to me
This land stretches out a thousand times)

MADAME SAVOIE & PRIEST:
(Overlapping.) HABITANTS, REGARDEZ LES BELLES FILLES DU ROI
LES BIJOUX DE NOTRE PATRIE
FILLETTES, CHOISISSEZ-VOUS UN BON MARI
DONNEZ-VOUS AU NOM DE LOUIS
(Habitants, look; the pretty daughters of the King
The jewels of our homeland
Girls, choose yourselves a good husband
Give yourselves in the name of Louis)

ALL: LES FILLES DU ROI
LES FILLES DU ROI
(The daughters of the King
the daughters of the King)

KATERI steps forward.

KATERI: *(Solo.)* WE WELCOME YOU TO SEE
WHAT THE WAMPUM SAYS WE COULD BE

CLAN MOTHER enters, drumming, and singing with a WOMAN OF THE LONGHOUSE.

ALL: AHHHH

CLAN MOTHER & FILLES:
(Overlapping.) WAY YAH HEY YAH WAY YO
WAY YAH HEY YO, WAY YAH HEY YO
WE NA MA HEY YAH HEY YO
WAY YAH HEY YO, WAY YAH HEY YO

JEAN-BAPTISTE & MARIE JEANNE:
(Overlapping.) SONHOWANEH KWA NE NE RATERIOS
AKWEKON NE IONKWAWATSIREH SEIATONHAWIS
TANON TANOWA IAKONTEHON NES
IETHINATON NE AHIONKI:IENAWASEH
(You have the soul of a fighter
You have our ancestors all right inside you
And while they may not be here
We will call to their ear)

CLAN MOTHER & FILLES:
(Overlapping.) WAY YAH HEY YAH WAY YO
WAY YAH HEY YO, WAY YAH HEY YO
WE NA MA HEY YAH HEY YO
WAY YAH HEY YO, WAY YAH HEY YO

FILLES: *(Overlapping.)* WE WON'T BE AFRAID OF THE ROAD AHEAD
WE ARE A PART OF IT ALL
LIVING THE LIVES THAT OUR FAMILIES DREAMT
WE'RE OFF, WE'RE OFF
WE'RE OFF, WE'RE OFF

ALL: *(Overlapping.)* WAY YAH HEY YAH WAY YO
WAY YAH HEY YO, WAY YAH HEY YO
WE NA MA HEY YAH HEY YO
WAY YAH HEY YO, WAY YAH HEY YO

KATERI: *(Overlapping.)* AND STILL I'LL GO
THERE'S MORE TO KNOW

(Solo.) WAY YAH HEY YAH WAY YO

KATERI stands alone on the shore, ready to build a beautiful future for herself and her people.

WAY YAH HEY YO, WAY YAH HEY YO

The end.

Indigenizing the Narrative of *Les Filles du Roi*

The process of developing *Les Filles du Roi* involved extensive research and consultation, including three trips to Kanien'kehá:ka (Mohawk) territory in southern Quebec and northern NY state.

On their first research trip in September 2016, Corey and Julie visited Kanien'kehá:ka Onkwawén:na Raotitióhkwa Language and Cultural Centre (http://korkahnawake.org, located in the Mohawk Territory of Kahnawà:ke south of Montreal), and the St Francis Xavier Mission (Kahnawà:ke Catholic Church). There they spoke with community members and learned that the settlement had its roots as a Jesuit mission, founded later than the dates of *Les Filles du Roi*. They also visited the Droulers-Tsiionhiakwatha archeological site in Saint-Anicet, QC (8 km south of the St Lawrence river), where they met with archeologist Michel Cadieux and toured a reconstructed 16th-century Kanien'kehá:ka village (http://www.sitedroulers.ca/site-en). Finally, they travelled to the Akwesasne Cultural Centre to meet Darren Bonaparte, a Mohawk historian, author, journalist, and artist. He is the creator of *The Wampum Chronicles*, a cultural history website, and is a frequent lecturer at schools, universities, museums, and festivals throughout the US and Canada. Corey and Julie spent a beautiful sunny afternoon with Darren, sitting at a picnic table outside the Native North American Travelling College on Cornwall Island (Akwesasne). They learned about the wampum and early treaties, and listened to stories (both documented and oral history) about first contact, events, and interactions between Mohawks and Europeans in the 17th century, and Kanien'kehá:ka communities on the St Lawrence River.

Throughout this first research trip, the focus was time and place: Corey and Julie were seeking guidance to connect the characters of Kateri and Jean-Baptiste to a specific area, and learning about the land on which they would have lived, the home to and from which they would have travelled to trade at Ville-Marie (now Montreal).

In June 2017, Corey and Julie made a second trip to Kanien'kehá:ka territory, this time to focus on the Kanien'kéha (Mohawk) language. It is their hope that *Les Filles du Roi* honours and contributes to ongoing language reclamation and cultural revitalization movements in the region (e.g., Kanien'kéha immersion schools). During this trip, they met with language speakers Kathy Herne and JoAnn Swamp at the Native North American Travelling College to talk about the project, and to begin the process of translating portions of dialogue into Kanien'kéha. This translation and language work – integrating both written Kanien'kéha and phonetics (to guide actors in learning the pronunciations) into the script – continued via long distance over the next eight months. Six different contributors from the community – all women – came together to do this, including the mother-daughter team of JoAnn and SueAnn Swamp. Sections of the script were discussed in language classes, by young people learning Kanien'kéha who worked together to translate and try out bits of dialogue.

Also during the creation and development process, production designer Marshall McMahen worked closely with Konwahonwá:wi Stacey, an artist from Kahnawa:ke Mohawk Territory in Quebec. She is Kanien'keha:ka Turtle clan, of the Haudenosaunee Confederacy. She shared her knowledge of traditional beadwork and quillwork patterns, and created the designs for all the beadwork seen in the show.

In April 2018, just before rehearsals for the world premiere production began, Corey and Julie made a third trip to Kanien'kehá:ka territory, this time accompanied by cast members Kaitlyn Yott, Raes Calvert, Chelsea Rose, and Laura Di Cicco, production designer Marshall McMahen, and movement director Patrice Bowler. This group visited the Droulers-Tsiionhiakwatha site, meeting again with archeologist Michel Cadieux and with site director Pascal Perron. The group learned that the area surrounding the site is unique; approximately a third of the neighbouring population is First Nations, a third French, and a third English. After the initial discovery of artifacts, all three of these communities came together to develop the site, the joint purpose being education. A white pine (symbol of the Tree of Peace / Haudenosaunee Confederacy) was gifted to the site and planted in the centre of the reconstructed village. As of spring 2018, all signage at the site is trilingual, with Kanien'kéha first, then French, then English.

During this trip, the *Les Filles du Roi* group also participated in two days of intensive language workshops at the Native North American Travelling College (NNATC) with Iawenta's (Mabel White), during which they focused on learning pronunciation, and on speaking the Kanien'kéha dialogue in an active and relationship-based way. They also learned about the ideology and worldview embedded in the language, and how it differs from an English / Western European framework.

On the evening of the second day, a community gathering was held, in which actors and creative team shared the *Les Filles du Roi* script, music, and designs with community members, and received feedback. A meal was also shared – including the traditional Three Sisters soup made of corn, beans, and squash, referenced by Kateri in the show. For this sharing, the NNATC loaned us a traditional Kanien'kehá:ka water drum for "Skén:nen Kowa," the Longhouse women's song.

This relationship with the community in Akwesasne is ongoing. We hope that, one day, we can share the full production with our friends and colleagues in Kanien'kehá:ka territory.

DEDICATORIA

A Douglas Zabdiel y Natasha Nery; mis amados hijos,
mis discípulos de toda la vida…

AGRADECIMIENTO

Al Rvdo. Douglas E. Mills Casablanca por su orientación pastoral y la oportunidad de servir en la escuela bíblica. ¡Gracias, mi amor!

CONTENIDO

PALABRAS DE LA AUTORA

Apreciados hermanas y hermanos

Todos tenemos un concepto de lo que es dar una clase, por la experiencia, el conocimiento y nuestra preferencia. En *Más que una clase* les comparto que la enseñanza bíblica tiene que ver esencialmente con nuestra práctica espiritual fuera de clase y en clase. En clase dirigimos al discípulo a un encuentro con Dios mediante el ejercicio estratégico del don de la enseñanza. Sin embargo, este es un proceso que tiene su inicio fuera de clase, cuando somos inspirados por nuestro encuentro interactivo con Dios, de tú a tú con el Maestro, dando como resultado un compromiso de acción personal y comunitaria.

Es luego que dirigimos al discípulo a dicho encuentro, fomentando la responsabilidad con su propia transformación y la respuesta a la enseñanza bíblica en su integración a la vida diaria. Este encuentro es interactivo entre el maestro y sus discípulos; entre los discípulos; y entre el Espíritu Santo y la persona. El estudio de la Biblia nos guía a comprometernos con su mensaje e integrarlo en nuestra vida mediante actos voluntarios inspirados por el encuentro con Dios. Por tanto, se proyecta como resultado un compromiso personal y comunitario para entender y practicar la enseñanza bíblica y progresar en el modo de vivir que agrada a Dios.[1]

Nuestra sociedad en crisis necesita interactuar con Dios para entender la fe cristiana, comprometerse continuamente con crecer en dicha fe y vivirla. Crisis es una palabra muy popular de estos días. Según la Real Academia Española, crisis significa situación mala o difícil.[2] Escuchamos hablar sobre la crisis gubernamental, económica, matrimonial, social, educativa, del individuo, y otras más. Es evidente que las condiciones de la sociedad que nos rodea y las comunidades específicas en que servimos, parecen ser cada vez más desastrosas (González, 2017). Esta realidad amenaza nuestra persona y la respuesta al llamado de Dios de servir, ya sea para contener o bajar su nivel en la ejecución. Sin embargo, la crisis es parte estructural de la educación porque la educación siempre tiene que innovar y adaptarse a nuevas situaciones (Touriñán, 2014). Crisis también significa cambio profundo y de consecuencias importantes en un proceso o una situación, o en la manera en que estos son apreciados. Por lo tanto, el escenario que estamos viviendo nos invita a concienciar sobre nuestra humanidad, reflexionar sobre nuestra identidad y cómo estamos sirviendo.

El propósito por el cual recibimos el don de Dios es para edificar el cuerpo de Cristo, lo cual tiene una meta común, según el escritor bíblico, hasta que todos lleguemos a estar unidos por la fe y el conocimiento del Hijo de Dios, y alcancemos la edad adulta, que corresponde a la plena madurez de Cristo.[3] El Dr. Justo L. González (González, 2006) lo expresó de manera concisa en su libro Tres meses en la escuela de la prisión cuando dijo: no quiere decir que cada uno por su cuenta llegue a la meta que se describe, sino más bien que todos juntos, como una realidad, como un solo cuerpo, lleguen a ser lo que allí se describe. Esta es una meta que

1. Efesios 4.15; 1 Tesalonicenses 4.1
2. Diccionario de la Lengua Española, 2019, https://www.rae.es.
3. Efesios 4.12-13

nos mantendrá a todos muy ocupados en la interacción con Dios, el compromiso y la acción correspondiente como respuesta.

En Más que una clase comparto algunas ideas prácticas para la buena mayordomía del don de la enseñanza, que aplican a una clase de cualquier edad. Las organicé en tres pasos que llamé el diseño de las **3P**: preparación, planificación y presentación. La preparación afirma el llamado divino y nuestra respuesta con un compromiso inspirado por el encuentro interactivo con Dios. En la planificación se seleccionan y organizan las actividades que componen la estrategia educativa e incluye una guía para su elaboración. Para ésta propongo el uso de las inteligencias múltiples como medio para ofrecer una clase interactiva, que facilite desarrollar una dinámica de integración de los discípulos y añada diversidad al proceso. También utilizo la asignación para comprometer al discípulo con su aprendizaje y responder al llamado de Dios. La presentación identifica otros detalles a considerar para que este encuentro sea bueno y edificante.

Aquí incluyo algunos conceptos que aparecen en mi libro Jesús, el Maestro: su plan educativo transformador (Nales, 2006). Además, algunos cambios al modelo para el plan de clase de siete pasos, que responde a las siguientes preguntas valoradas personalmente como guía para realizar la tarea:

Paso 1: *¿Cómo comienzo?* = Presentación
Paso 2: *¿Cómo logro el interés del discípulo?* = Motivación
Paso 3: *¿Cómo lo voy a hacer?* = Estrategia de enseñanza
Paso 4: *¿Cómo actualizo la enseñanza?* = Relación con la vida diaria
Paso 5: *¿Qué aprendieron?* = Evaluación
Paso 6: *¿Qué estudiaremos en la próxima clase?* = Motivación para el próximo estudio
Paso 7: *¿Cómo termino?* = Oración

La idea de los siete pasos tiene relación con el inicio de mi servicio en la escuela bíblica. Solo tenía 15 años de edad cuando mi pastor, Jorge Luis Pabón Moraza, me pidió que fuera maestra de la niñez con edad preescolar. Mi experiencia de creyente era de un año y no tenía conocimiento alguno sobre cómo enseñar. Aunque ya sabía que Dios daba dones, no entendía cómo eso funcionaba ni imaginaba lo que Dios quería para mi vida. Estaba aprendiendo a amar a Dios y quería servirle. Busqué un libro que me orientará por pasos cómo ser maestra de Biblia, pero no lo encontré. Agradezco a Dios por la diligencia del Pastor al coordinar mi integración como maestra con la ayuda de la hermana Malén, quien me dio ejemplo y dirección. Ciertamente el Espíritu Santo me ayuda a entender la necesidad de comprometerme día a día con el llamado de Dios, de vivir su verdad y procurar crecer en Cristo.[4]

Aunque aún me surgen las mismas preguntas cuando estoy preparando la clase, mi propuesta actual es que su contenido sea reagrupado en solo tres pasos: *Inicio*, *Desarrollo* y *Cierre*. ¿Qué motivó la reagrupación? Mi pastor actual fue el agente motivador. Ahora le cuento la otra historia. Un día el Rvdo. Douglas E. Mills Casablanca me compartió una actividad que estaba planificando para los maestros de escuela bíblica con mi participación. La actividad tenía doble propósito: (1) orientar sobre un proyecto nuevo, la Historia; y (2) compartir una estrategia sencilla para dar la clase. La Historia estudiaba la Biblia completa como un relato ininterrumpido acerca de Dios; un proyecto interesantísimo que usa la Nueva Versión Internacional (NVI). El reto era organizar el currículo con la duración de 31 semanas, pero solo una reunión al mes, de aproximadamente 50 minutos. Esto implicaba que cada reunión cubriría una historia con diversos pasajes bíblico. Sobre la segunda actividad, el pastor Mills recomendó que presentara una clase en tres pasos para facilitarle a quien enseñaba el recordar

4. Efesios 4.15

la estructura que le daría dirección. El contenido del proyecto y la estructura de tres pasos no significaban menos dedicación en la preparación del maestro, sino que demandaban una práctica estratégica. Entonces usé los recursos de la educación.

Esta experiencia me hizo recordar a la Dra. Aida Besançon, cuando fue mi profesora del curso El Nuevo Testamento y la mujer. Ella narró a la clase cómo se originó la enseñanza del hebreo en una escuela bíblica, algo poco común. Explicó que en la iglesia había muchas personas que deseaban un reto mayor en el estudio de la Biblia y así lo expresaron al pastor. En ese tiempo ella era miembro de dicha congregación y enseñaba hebreo en un Seminario en los EEUU. El pastor identificó que tenía el recurso para atender la necesidad particular expresada. Entonces, compartió a la hermana Besançon su visión de un grupo pequeño en la escuela bíblica para el estudio de la biblia en el idioma hebreo y le solicitó su servicio. Ella confesó a la clase que esto significó un gran reto personal, pues no era la población a la que acostumbraba enseñar. Sin embargo, aceptó aprender aquello que necesario, estuvo disponible para hacer los ajustes en su estrategia y caminar como el Maestro, sirviendo por su amor a Dios.[5]

Los pastores mencionados identificaron la necesidad que tenían que atender y buscaron el recurso para hacerlo. Cuando aceptamos la invitación a servir lo que Dios nos dio y nos comprometemos a hacerlo bien, seremos una feliz bendición (frase del pastor Mills que hice mía por la integración personal y comunitaria). Es normal que lo innovador nos cause resistencia mental, algún tipo de temor. También nos recordará que somos discípulos y servidores, que seguimos aprendiendo para servir mejor como buenos administradores de la gracia de Dios. Como dice el escritor bíblico de Romanos 12.4-5: los miembros del cuerpo no tienen la misma función, pero tienen el fin común de trabajar para que

5. Juan 14.31

el cuerpo sea cuerpo. Contamos con la ayuda del Espíritu Santo y el modelo del Maestro para continuar en nuestro crecimiento a lo largo de la vida.

Ante nosotros tenemos el llamado a servir a un nivel que refleje la verdad del amor de Dios y de ser estratégicos con pertinencia al llamado. Es menester afirmar para qué sirve la educación cristiana y usar los recursos necesarios para cumplir su propósito. Ciertamente la Biblia nos manda a usar el don recibido para servir a otros, administrando fielmente la gracia de Dios en sus diversas formas.[6] El énfasis del apóstol Pedro es en la responsabilidad que tenemos hacia los demás de ministrar a otros la gracia de Dios que actúa en nosotros. Él nos relaciona con la imagen del administrador en el mundo antiguo, quien le servía a otros de lo que no le pertenecía a él, así nos dice que debemos ser buenos administradores porque lo que servimos es nada menos que los diferentes dones de Dios (Green, 1993). Recibimos y experimentamos la gracia de Dios para compartirla de tal manera y en tal grado como Él nos amó. Entonces, respondemos con nuestro servicio por amor y con amor; no por protagonismo o por obligación, sino como una extensión y reflejo de la gracia de Dios que ya hemos experimentamos.

El texto bíblico citado es principalmente según la *Biblia de Estudio Dios Habla Hoy* (1994), tercera edición, Sociedades Bíblicas Unidas. Esa versión es una traducción directa de los textos en los idiomas originales: hebreo, arameo y griego. Usa un lenguaje sencillo para que el lector pueda comprender; por eso, la traducción se llama "versión popular". Reconozco el lenguaje inclusivo. Éste se demuestra por el uso alterno del género femenino y masculino, a veces con el colectivo y plural, con el fin de facilitar su lectura. Utilizo el término discípulos para evocar el significado que le dio Jesús, quien invitaba y desafiaba a unirse a sus seguidores,

6. 1 Pedro 4.10

dispuestos a vivir a la altura de sus enseñanzas y valores (Pagán, 2012). También, utilizo el término transformación que significa la nueva naturaleza y formación continua del creyente para reflejar la gloria del Señor.[7] El testimonio vivo del arrepentimiento que tuvo inicio en nuestro corazón y es visible en la práctica de vivir la voluntad de Dios con la ayuda del Espíritu Santo. El término aprendizaje lo uso para nombrar la adquisición por la práctica de una espiritualidad que reconoce el valor social y espiritual de una adoración integral, refiriéndose a la transformación.[8]

Te invito a disfrutar de una dinámica reflexiva antes de iniciar la lectura, completando el formulario *Autoevaluación.* El resultado te ayudará a determinar cuál es el área que necesitas mejorar, de acuerdo a lo que compartimos en el diseño de las 3P. ¡Qué la lectura te bendiga y sea útil para realizar tu servicio!

Tu hermana en Cristo y compañera en el servicio,

Nereida

7. 2 Corintios 3.18; Efesios 4.24.
8. Romanos 12.1-2

AUTOEVALUACIÓN

Práctica del don de enseñar según el diseño de las 3P

Instrucciones: Haga una marca de cotejo (√) en la columna "¿Con qué frecuencia?" para indicar la frecuencia con que realiza cada actividad. Utilice la siguiente escala: (1) Muy poco; (2) Frecuente; (3) Siempre. Conteste con honestidad.*

	¿Con qué frecuencia?		
I. Preparación	**1**	**2**	**3**
1. Comparto a solas con Dios diariamente.			
2. Consulto diversas versiones de la Biblia.			
3. Busco relacionar la clase que daré con mi realidad.			
4. Oro por mí y mis discípulos.			
5. Practico una educación continua para mejorar el servicio de enseñar, tales como: talleres de capacitación, lecturas relacionadas, mentoría.			
6. Cuido de mi bienestar holístico.			
7. Vivo la unidad y edificación de la comunidad de fe.			
8. Practico los valores del reino que aprendí del Maestro.			
9. Doy seguimiento mi discipulado con una lectura sistemática de la Biblia.			
II. Planificación de la clase:	**1**	**2**	**3**
10. Comienzo el estudio de la clase con una semana de anticipación.			
11. Hago mi plan de clase como guía para la presentación.			
12. Pienso en las necesidades, etapa de desarrollo e intereses de mis discípulos.			
13. Selecciono una estrategia de enseñanza diferente a la clase pasada.			
14. Incluyo diversas y diferentes actividades de aprendizaje.			
15. Creo una actividad para aplicar la enseñanza a la vida diaria.			
16. Realizo la actividad de aplicación del texto a mi vida.			
17. Planifico una asignación para comprometer con el aprendizaje.			
18. Adquiero los recursos que necesito con anticipación al día de la clase.			
19. Repaso la clase el día antes.			
III. Presentación de la clase:	**1**	**2**	**3**
20. Saludo con alegría a toda la clase, incluyendo a las visitas.			
21. Comienzo con una actividad que motive el interés de todos por la clase.			
22. Informo el propósito de la clase y cómo la conduciremos.			
23. Uso la Biblia en clase.			
24. Promuevo la participación activa de la clase.			
25. Escucho a los discípulos para enfocar la clase de manera efectiva.			
26. Cuido el ambiente de la clase para que predominen los valores del reino.			
27. Dirijo a la reflexión sobre el tema estudiado.			
28. Comprometo al discípulo con su transformación.			
29. Invito a la clase a conocer al Salvador y a vivir en amistad con Dios.			
30. Termino con una oración.			
Reflexión:			

*A mayor frecuencia más adecuado. Haga el cómputo y reflexione sobre su resultado.

1

PREPARACIÓN

"Y él mismo concedió a unos ser... maestros"
EFESIOS 4.11

La primera **P** se refiere a la disposición de la persona para un encuentro con Dios con el fin de recibir y entender la enseñanza, comprometerse con su propia transformación a lo largo de su vida, actuar en respuesta al mensaje de Dios y participar intencionalmente en la transformación del discípulo. La *preparación* comienza con el reconocimiento de nuestra identidad como siervos de Dios. Requiere una cita íntima, muy íntima con el que nos llamó, nuestro Señor. Compararla con una cita no sólo identifica un momento, sino la disposición para encontrarnos con Dios y ponernos de acuerdo con él.

En una ocasión alguien expresó con desilusión que la clase bíblica de su iglesia no le parecía conectada con la realidad; el mensaje era que todo estaba bien, no había dificultades, malestares o desazón, pues la vida del creyente era perfecta. Confesó que necesitaba una palabra con significado para su vida, escuchar la voz de Dios que le diera dirección para vivir el consejo divino en medio de su realidad, donde las cosas no iban tan bien ni era perfecta. Deseaba dialogar con el texto en su horizonte actual, entrar en una dimensión más profunda y pertinente para comprender las posibilidades de vida, abrazar la misma, y aprender a resistir su aflicción, como dice el Dr. Ediberto López Rodríguez en su libro Para que comprendiesen las Escrituras (2003). Ciertamente la educación cristiana no se circunscribe a quien enseña en la escuela bíblica (Mejías, 2019). La iglesia utiliza una diversidad de escenarios para educar y cumplir su misión, conforme a los dones recibidos por cada miembro según Cristo repartió.[1] Sin embargo, aquí hablamos solo del servicio de escuela bíblica.

Quien enseña no fue llamado a impresionar al discípulo con palabras rítmicas, la demostración de mucho conocimiento o de una gran personalidad. Tampoco a entretener ni anestesiar al discípulo ante los conflictos de su realidad existencial. Fuimos llamados por Dios para ejercer el don que el Señor quiso darnos; a realizar un trabajo de servicio para la edificación del cuerpo de Cristo.[2] Así guiar a la transformación por el poder de la palabra, que capacita para vivir el amor de Dios en medio de cualesquiera sean las circunstancias; de manera que gocen la vida abundante y libertad que Jesús compró, disfruten esa gracia de Dios y sean reflejo del amor de Dios en palabras y hechos.

El apóstol Pablo expresó *que hay diferentes maneras de servir, pero todas por encargo de un mismo Señor… y un mismo Espíritu, dando a cada persona lo que a él mejor le parece.*[3] Entonces, la idea de que sirvamos en la enseñanza se le ocurrió al mismo Dios, tuvo su origen en la mente de Dios. Ahora bien, eso es solo el comienzo. Necesitamos armonizar el poder de Dios con nuestra humanidad, lo cual requiere nuestro compromiso espiritual. ¿Vio la primera película de *Iron man, basada en Marvel Comics*? Cuando el personaje se puso por primera vez la vestimenta de hierro no sabía manejarla. Requirió varios ajustes para un mejor

1. Efesios 4.7
2. Efesios 4.11-12
3. 1 Corintios 12.1,11

funcionamiento y mucha práctica, lo que resultó en su transformación. Nosotros debemos aprender a usar el don de Dios y estar atentos para identificar dónde nos toca hacer los ajustes para su buen funcionamiento.

En la iglesia primitiva era tenido en alta estima quien enseñaba (Deiros, 1992). Por lo que no eran pocos los que querían ser reconocidos como maestros, tuviesen o no la capacidad. Sin embargo, el apóstol Santiago escribió: ..no haya entre ustedes tantos maestros, pues ya saben que quienes enseñamos seremos juzgados con más severidad.[4] Esto no lo dijo para desalentar el ejercicio de la enseñanza, sino para llamarle la atención a los que querían enseñar sin entender bien lo que enseñaban ni el grado de responsabilidad que esto involucra. Lo que el Apóstol destaca es la importancia de vivir una integridad personal y comunitaria, pues podemos hacer daño en lugar de bien. Los maestros verdaderos saben que tienen que ordenar toda su vida de acuerdo a la voluntad de Dios y esforzarse para vivir según el carácter de Dios, y así enseñar lo mismo a toda la comunidad de fe. De hecho, el Apóstol se incluyó también en el grupo a quien dirigía su exhortación, dejando claro la conciencia de su humanidad. Es que la práctica de la vida cristiana que este llamado impone, requiere la humildad de un espíritu enseñable por Dios para aprender a aprender. En este proceso podríamos encontrarnos con la necesidad de desaprender algo que no corresponde al modelo de nuestro Maestro Jesús, que estén ocupando el espacio de su enseñanza. Entonces, tenemos que vaciarnos para estar disponible completamente, ser discípulos del Maestro, y practicar su enseñanza.

Ciertamente el reino de Dios no consiste en palabras, sino en poder.[5] Y su poder es el don de Dios que evidencia su amor. Este amor no es cómplice del *Poema del Renunciamiento* de José Ángel

4. Santiago 3.1; 1 Corintios 12.29; Hechos 13.1

5. 1 Corintios 4.20

Buesa cuando dice: Pasarás por mi vida sin saber que pasaste. Pasarás en silencio por mi amor y, al pasar, fingiré una sonrisa como un dulce contraste del dolor de quererte... y jamás lo sabrás. Según el análisis del poema por Susana Marín (2014), éste habla de una persona que declara cuán importante es para su mundo aquella a quien ama; sin embargo, no existe una relación de amor equilibrada porque su amor es silente. Aquí el que ama se privó de ser amado al no decir que amaba, pues pensó que era imposible que su amor fuera correspondido.

Por el contrario, Dios hizo notorio ante todo el mundo cuando vino a nosotros, él marcó la historia con su demostración de amor.[6] No calló su amor ni fingió, dejándonos ignorantes sobre él, sin darnos la oportunidad de disfrutarlo. En su lugar, Dios salió a buscarnos cargado de regalos útiles que nos hablan de un amor fiel y sin fingimiento, quedándose con nosotros por siempre para enseñarnos a amarle de la misma manera. Aún en esos momentos donde todo lo que vemos es oscuridad y no sentimos su amor presente, él está ahí con nosotros como el Buen Pastor, haciendo notorio su amor activo.[7]

El primer don que recibimos de Dios fue la salvación. Su amor libertador nos rescató de la esclavitud, venciendo todo poder del mal, el pecado, la muerte y al mismo diablo.[8] Su presencia es palpable con la acción del Espíritu Santo, quien nos ayuda en nuestra debilidad; que ruega a Dios por nosotros cuando no sabemos orar como es debido, y lo hace de modo tan especial que no hay palabras para expresarlo.[9] Además, nos capacitó para seguir creciendo en todo y parecernos a él.[10] Su llamado es que nos acerquemos

6. Juan 1

7. Salmos 23.4

8. Efesios 2.1-10; 4.7-13

9. Romanos 8.26

10. Efesios 2.15

con confianza al Dios amoroso para tener la experiencia de su amor fiel.[11]

Recibimos el don para ser capacitados y completamente preparados, no porque ya lo seamos. Es para que todos los que formamos la iglesia, que es su cuerpo, estemos capacitados para servir y edificar.[12] El apóstol Pablo nos ayuda a comprender mejor la perfección en el contexto cristiano cuando explica el resultado de la palabra de Dios en la vida del creyente: Todo lo que está escrito en la Biblia es el mensaje de Dios, y es útil para enseñar a la gente, para ayudarla y corregirla, y para mostrarle cómo debe vivir. De ese modo, los servidores de Dios estarán completamente entrenados y preparados para hacer el bien.[13]

Entonces, como buenos discípulos estudiemos la vida de nuestro Maestro para aprender de Él, seguir su ejemplo, imitarlo. Este estudio personal debe ser continuo a lo largo de nuestra vida, una y otra vez.

COMPROMISO INSPIRADO POR EL ENCUENTRO INTERACTIVO CON DIOS

La palabra dada, la obligación contraída definen compromiso de manera popular, según la Real Academia Española. Una mirada a nuestro alrededor podría llevarnos a pensar que el compromiso parece ser una palabra en desuso en este tiempo. Algunas de la razones podrían ser el aumento de las rupturas de matrimonios, la ausencia paterna en la vida de los hijos, la condición pobre del país por causa del enriquecimiento de sus líderes, la ausencia en el templo de quien es parte del cuerpo de Cristo, la falta de servir el don recibido, entre otros en la lista.

Veamos la vida del Maestro según el Evangelio de Marcos para identificar las prácticas que evidencian su compromiso de servicio.

11. Hebreos 4.16
12. Efesios 4.12
13. 2 Timoteo 3.16-17 – Traducción en Lenguaje Actual (TLA)

La mayoría de los teólogos creen que el Evangelio de Marcos fue el primero que se redactó. Éste comienza diferente a los otros Evangelios sinópticos; no habla de la infancia del Maestro, sino que va directo a presentar el comienzo de su ministerio. Destaca con mucha frecuencia que parte muy importante de la actividad de Jesús era la de enseñar a la multitud, y de manera particular al grupo de discípulos (4.33-34).[14] Marcos presenta la vida del Maestro en dos etapas: su identidad (1-8) y su misión (9-16). Identifiqué las siguientes prácticas que manifiestan su compromiso de servicio:

1. Vivía la plenitud del Espíritu de Dios

Escuchó el llamado de Dios y le creyó.[15] Se dejó llevar, aceptó la dirección del Espíritu de Dios, confiando en su acompañamiento y cuidado.[16] La gente se admiraba de cómo les enseñaba porque lo hacía con plena autoridad y no como los maestros de la ley.[17] Él vivía su enseñanza. Su vida fue la principal estrategia de enseñanza para motivar a los discípulos a participar del reino de Dios, a creer lo que les decía y que se comprometieran con la trasformación de su vida. El enemigo también reconocía la plenitud del Espíritu de Dios en él.[18]

2. Compartía a solas con Dios

El Maestro creaba su espacio a solas con Dios aunque su diario vivir fuera muy ocupado. A veces Jesús se levantaba de madrugada, cuando todavía estaba oscuro y salía de la ciudad para ir a orar a un lugar solitario, tranquilo.[19] En otras ocasiones, hizo que

14. La Biblia de Estudio Dios Habla Hoy, 1994.
15. Marcos 1.11,14,15
16. Marcos 1.12
17. Marcos 1.22;12.38-40
18. Marcos 1.24
19. Marcos 1.35

sus discípulos salieran antes que él hacia el lugar planificado, se encargaba de despedir a la gente y luego se iba al cerro a orar.[20] Su comunión con Dios le dio la confianza de servir sabiendo que contaba con el respaldo de Dios.[21] Cuando experimentó la tristeza y la angustia, buscó el apoyo con los más cercanos, pero no dejó su práctica personal de orar.[22] En su oración abrió su corazón a Dios y le pidió con toda la confianza e intimidad con la que un hijo le pide a su padre.[23] Jesús conocía que la petición a Dios libra de la ansiedad que impide seguir adelante porque se ejercita el músculo de la fe, al saber a quién ir y reconocer su acompañamiento.[24] Y cuando sintió que Dios lo había abandonado, se lo expresó con sinceridad y todavía con el reconocimiento de ser su Dios.[25]

3. Ejercitaba la voluntad divina

Jesús entendía cuál era la misión recibida de Dios. Llevaba a cabo la voluntad de Dios de anunciar el mensaje y afirmaba a sus discípulos que para esto había salido.[26] Aprendió a sentirse cómodo en su tarea de enseñar, de hablarles aunque se reunía alrededor de él mucha gente.[27] Esto no fue un camino fácil. Él se enojó con los que le rodeaban, se entristeció por sus actitudes. [28] Se asombraba de la incredulidad, pero seguía enseñando.[29] Además, afirmaba en su oración que quería hacer lo que Dios quería.[30]

20. Marcos 6.46
21. Marcos 5.40-41;6.41
22. Marcos 14.32-39
23. Marcos 14.36
24. Marcos 11.22
25. Marcos 15.34
26. Marcos 1.38
27. Marcos 4.1
28. Marcos 3.5; 8.12
29. Marcos 6.6
30. Marcos 14.35-36

4. Cuidaba su bienestar

Jesús no canceló su humanidad y creaba estrategias ante los obstáculos que enfrentaba. Por ejemplo, luego de la experiencia de tener una multitud que se echaba encima de él para tocarlo porque querían ser sanados, hizo los arreglos para evitar que esto volviera a suceder. Les encargó a sus discípulos que le tuvieran lista una barca.[31] También, comprendió que su tiempo estaba muy comprometido a causa de tanta gente que iba y venía. A veces no tenía tiempo para comer. Así que les dijo a sus discípulos vamos nosotros solos a descansar un poco en un lugar tranquilo, apartado.[32] Es cierto que a veces su gestión no le resultó porque se encontró nuevamente de cara con la necesidad de otros y la compasión que proviene del carácter de Dios lo condujo a servir por amor y en respuesta a su llamado.[33] Sin embargo, esto no le hizo olvidar el compromiso con su persona y nuevamente creó el espacio.[34]

Estas prácticas de Jesús evidencian una vida interactiva con Dios, sobre la base sólida de su identidad y su determinación de amar al Padre, enfrentando las dificultades de la vida y cuidándose día a día para cumplir la voluntad divina. En el momento de **Preparación** afirmamos nuestra identidad como discípulos del Maestro y llamados a enseñar. En este paso Dios sigue haciendo una buena obra en nosotros para llevarnos a un buen fin.[35]

El Maestro nos enseñó a vivir en constante comunicación con Dios para cumplir el llamado de servicio. Su práctica estratégica de mantener el contacto con Dios, en cualquiera que fuera la realidad que viviera, demostró su determinación en seguir hacia la

31. Marcos 3.9
32. Marcos 6.30-32
33. Mateo 6.34
34. Marcos 6.45-47
35. Filipenses 1.6

culminación de su obra. Si algún día tuviéramos la necesidad de recibir la oración de la comunidad de fe, pidámosla. Si estamos pasando por un momento difícil, es probable que nos sintamos afectados emocionalmente, pero Dios tiene disponible su paz que es medicina divina para guardar nuestro corazón y pensamientos.[36]

Como portavoz de su mensaje, Dios tiene mucho que decirnos y nosotros mucho que escuchar y aprender. Por tanto, tenemos que ser intencional para crear un tiempo a solas con Dios. Practiquemos como Jesús hablarle a Dios porque él escucha; y escuchar a Dios porque Él también nos habla. ¿Cuál de estas prácticas le parece viable?:

1. Determine la hora de oración. Por ejemplo, el salmista dijo: de mañana escuchas mi voz; muy temprano te expongo mi caso, y quedo esperando tu respuesta (Salmos 5.3). Alguien dijo que si oramos de mañana, luego de una noche de descanso en que las preocupaciones se aquietan, y la mente aún no está cargada por las agitaciones del día, percibiremos mejor la respuesta divina; será un buen comienzo.
2. Anote en su agenda o ponga una alarma para su cita diaria con Dios.
3. Llegue más temprano al trabajo para hacer su devocional personal; evitará el tapón y aprovechará el tiempo con Dios.
4. Apague el radio del carro y hable con Dios durante el camino.
5. Salga a caminar; ejercitará su cuerpo y se conectará con Dios mientras disfruta de la naturaleza.
6. Esté siempre preparado para tomar notas sobre lo que Dios le dice, ya sea en una libreta o en el celular.

36. Filipenses 4.6-7

7. Mantenga la comunión con Dios en toda hora y todo lugar. No tiene que esperar a encontrar el espacio y el lugar para tirarse de rodillas; hágalo en su mente, con todo su corazón. Siga el consejo bíblico: *oren en todo momento*.[37]

Oremos como dice el cántico de Jesús Adrián Romero: "Sumérgeme en el río de tu Espíritu". La invitación de Dios es pasar al otro nivel, porque el río de Dios creció tanto para bendecirnos que no podemos continuar caminando, sino cruzar a nado.[38] Mantengámonos inspirados por un encuentro interactivo con Dios, viviendo el discipulado; pasar tiempo con él nos ayudará a reconocer su voz en el estudio de la clase y recibir su dirección.

ESTUDIO DE LA CLASE

Como resultado de las investigaciones en las neurociencias, hoy se conoce más sobre cómo funciona el cerebro humano y su aplicabilidad a la sala de clases. Si el componente psicológico y el sociológico son importantes, no es menos importante el componente biológico, el cerebro especialmente, que es donde ocurre el aprendizaje de conocimiento (Álvarez, 2006). Enseñamos a personas, por lo cual es importante la aportación de aquellos conocimientos específicos del saber humano.

Por ejemplo, las investigaciones en las neurociencias descubrieron que el cerebro humano asimila poco a poco. Estos descubrimientos señalan la importancia de que dediquemos un tiempo adecuado al estudio de nuestra clase para entenderla y crear la oportunidad de pensar bien sobre la estrategia que ayudará mejor

37. 1 Tesalonicenses 5.17

38. Ezequiel 47

a los discípulos para que también la entiendan. El Creador sabe cómo el ser humano funciona y por eso utiliza las experiencias cotidianas para ministrarnos sobre el tema a enseñar. Cuando iniciamos el estudio de la clase con una semana de anticipación, permitimos al cerebro asimilar el mensaje de Dios para nuestra vida y comprender cuál es el mensaje que Dios quiere dar a los discípulos. Si en la lectura bíblica nosotros no vemos ni entendemos cuál es el mensaje de Dios a nuestra vida, tampoco seremos buenos guías para que lo vean y lo entiendan los discípulos. El maestro que está conectado durante la semana con el texto bíblico que compartirá en clase, captará diariamente la ayuda de Dios a través del Espíritu Santo.

Distribuir el estudio entre varios días de la semana ayudará el cerebro para hacer las conexiones e integrar la información. ¿Cuánto tiempo es necesario para cada día? Eso es relativo, cada persona determinará el tiempo que necesite. La lectura bíblica requiere oír, estudiar, meditar, memorizar y vivir su enseñanza. Lo cierto es que la disciplina de estudio lleva a una entrega total al Espíritu Santo. Durante el transcurso de la semana pensaremos en la estrategia y los recursos necesarios para la presentación.

¿Cómo distribuir el estudio de la clase? Identifiquemos los días de la semana que son viables para crear un tiempo apartado con dicho enfoque. Es necesario empezar al inicio de la semana para integrar poco a poco, tal como funciona el cerebro. Por ejemplo, si la clase es domingo, en nuestra agenda semanal crearemos un tiempo para las siguientes actividades que son presentadas en dos alternativas: Figura 1 y 2:

Figura 1: Semana de estudio en cinco días

Lunes	Martes	Miércoles	Jueves	Sábado
• Lectura	• Identifica los términos	• Estudio del texto	• Diálogo con el texto para su aplicación	• Repaso

Figura 2: Semana de estudio en tres días

Lunes	Miércoles	Sábado
• Lectura • Identificar los términos	• Estudio del texto • Diálogo con el texto para su aplicación	• Repaso

LECTURA

Tengamos un momento de oración antes de leer las Escrituras. Entonces leamos el texto bíblico relacionado a la clase; disfrutemos la lectura, saboreemos lo que dice. Luego, leamos el contexto de la lectura bíblica, al menos el capítulo anterior y el posterior. A veces es necesario leer un poco más para entender lo que nos cuenta. Leamos diferentes versiones. Por ejemplo, Nueva Versión Internacional (NVI), Dios habla hoy (DHH), Traducción en Lenguaje Actual (TLA), Biblia de Jerusalén, La Biblia Latinoamericana, King James versión (KJV). No tienen que ser todas las mencionadas, la idea es que demos preferencia a las Biblias que se identifican como traducción directa de los textos originales: hebreo, arameo y griego. Además, leamos la versión Reina-Valera (RVR1960), la cual probablemente tendrán muchos el día de la clase.

Gracias a la Biblia App de YouVersion (www.bible.com, youversion.com), tenemos acceso en forma gratuita a diferentes versiones de la Biblia para uso personal o para uso interno de la organización sin fines de lucro. Esta herramienta es muy útil para la preparación, planificación e, inclusive, como una actividad tecnológica en la presentación de la clase. Dios hizo otra provisión para que seamos el creyente maduro y completo que quiere. Damos gracias a Dios por la hermandad capacitada con la tecnología que trabajó responsablemente y con amor para que fuera una herramienta eficiente (YouVersion o Life.Church). Comparar las diversas versiones, de esta manera rápida que tenemos accesible, facilitará el estudio personal. Definitivamente es una bendición cuando cada uno sirve el don recibido. El dio dones a cada uno y cuando servimos como buenos administradores somos partícipes del crecimiento de la iglesia en el conocimiento de Dios y la unidad de la fe.

También es una experiencia enriquecedora cuando hacemos la lectura del texto bíblico en su forma original, sin división de capítulos ni versículos.[39] Por ejemplo, podremos disfrutarla con las dos ediciones bíblicas *Los libros de la Biblia:* (1) *La Historia del Pacto*, y (2) el *Nuevo Testamento*. La Historia del Pacto sigue muy de cerca la estructura antigua de las Escrituras hebreas: la Ley, los Profetas y los Escritos.[40] El Nuevo Testamento presenta este antiguo concepto de los cuatro evangelios.[41] Esta estructura evita que veamos unidades de pensamientos más largos y cortos dentro de los libros bíblicos. Como dice el Dr. Justo L. González, lo que en la versión Dios Habla Hoy se nos da gota a gota como para que podamos asimilarlo, en el original es un «Niágara» cuyo torrente nos lleva consigo... léalo de un golpe... le ayudará a sentirlo y vivirlo (González, 1997). Repitamos la lectura. Leamos una y otra vez, disfrutémosla.

IDENTIFICACIÓN DE LOS TÉRMINOS

Marquemos cada término que nos llame la atención, tales como: nombre de personas, de lugares y vocabulario que no conozcamos. Anotemos los sinónimos encontrados en las diversas versiones, esto lo integraremos luego en la clase. Observemos si el texto da énfasis a una palabra, repitiendo la misma en diversos versículos. Hagamos una lista de los términos que seleccionamos para

39. La división por capítulos se incluyó en el siglo XIII; y la de versículos, en el siglo XVI d.C.
40. La Historia del Pacto (2011) por Bíblica, Inc. Los Libros de la Biblia.
41. Nuevo Testamento (2011) por Bíblica, Inc. Los libros de la Biblia.

estudiar. Busquemos información que nos ayudará a su comprensión. Utilicemos la misma libreta para la preparación de todas las clases. De esta manera mantendrá sus estudios juntos y podrá utilizarlos como referencias futuras. Si será la misma que nos guiará el día de la clase, entonces consideremos algo manejable y presentable.

Ciertamente necesitaremos recursos que nos ayuden en el estudio de los términos para la comprensión bíblica. Por ejemplo, comentarios bíblicos, diccionarios bíblicos, diccionario del idioma, concordancias de los idiomas usados en la Biblia, sinopsis de los Evangelios, libros de geografía bíblica, entre otros que estimemos necesario. También es necesario que cultivemos la práctica de leer artículos sobre diversos temas, tales como: teología, educación, sicología, salud, ciencias, tecnología; siempre recordaremos alguna una lectura que será un recurso útil para la clase. Mantengamos actualizado nuestros recursos de referencia, de tal manera que nos faciliten extraer los tesoros nuevos de los tesoros antiguos que hay en la Biblia, como dice el Dr. Ediberto López. (López, 2003). La experiencia de identificar los términos y examinarlos tomará uno o dos días; entonces, ya será mitad de semana.

ESTUDIO DEL TEXTO BÍBLICO

En esta ocasión vamos a descomponer el texto mediante el proceso de interpretación bíblica, el cual es un diálogo con el texto, con Dios y con uno mismo. La interpretación bíblica incluye la exégesis y la hermenéutica. El concepto exégesis proviene de dos palabras griegas que significan "dirigir hacia fuera" para interpretar lo que el texto significó originalmente. El concepto de hermenéutica está orientado a la interpretación potencial del texto bíblico para nuestro contexto y su aplicación. En el estudio del texto bíblico nos referimos a la exégesis. Esta dinámica dirigirá su enseñanza para que sea bíblicamente informada y ofrezca una aplicación actual para la vida diaria; de la aplicación hablaremos más adelante.

El obstáculo más serio para hacer una interpretación bíblica es la distancia entre el texto y nosotros, entre la Biblia y nuestro mundo; por ejemplo, lingüística, histórica, sociológica, cultural y tecnológica (López, 2003). Explica el Dr. López que el texto tiene un *detrás*, un *en*, y un *delante*. *Detrás* del texto están todas las preguntas sobre su trasfondo histórico y social que es necesario localizar para comprender lo que el texto pudo significar en su contexto inicial; el *en* del texto se refiere a la sensibilidad literaria que necesitamos para la comprensión adecuada, al ver todos los asuntos literarios y estructurales presentes; y con el *delante* de texto, está la autonomía que gana el texto en un nuevo contexto, con nuevos lectores. Aquí nos corresponde estudiar el trasfondo histórico y social y los asuntos literarios y estructurales del texto.

Ciertamente la tarea de interpretación bíblica requiere la responsabilidad ética que implica leer e interpretar (López, 2003). ¿Cuáles son las respuestas bíblicas a sus preguntas? El texto habla de experiencias pasadas y necesitamos reconocer los elementos internos, identificar las ideologías aceptables de su contexto, aquellas que no sean aceptables para el lector de hoy, y que requieren considerar la Biblia en su sentido más completo. Ejemplo de esas ideologías aceptables en su contexto, diferente al de hoy, son: patriarcal, la xenofobia, la esclavitud, la injusticia.

Aunque el contexto en que se escribió el texto no sea el mismo del lector de hoy, Dios tiene una palabra de vida nueva para nuestro tiempo. Esto podría sonar difícil de hacer si nos quedamos pensando que su contenido incluye diversos géneros literarios, escritos por muchos autores de diferentes culturas, tiempos y varios idiomas. Ciertamente el texto presenta experiencias pasadas, pero el lector viene al texto con sus preguntas y experiencias del presente.[42] Esto lo trabajaremos en el próximo tema, el diálogo con el texto para su aplicación.

DIÁLOGO CON EL TEXTO PARA SU APLICACIÓN

Aquí buscamos tener un encuentro interactivo con Dios a través del texto, lo que requiere nuestro enfoque y receptividad para escuchar lo que Dios quiere que aprendamos hoy. Esto significa que debemos darnos una buena sentada como María a los pies del Maestro.[43] Cuando lo escuchamos y le hacemos preguntas, recibimos un mensaje pertinente que entendemos y podemos comunicar. Lucas 2.46 cuenta que Jesús tuvo esa experiencia en el Templo cuando dialogó con los maestros. Jesús estaba en medio de ellos como quien está aprendiendo, no como maestro; escuchaba y hacía preguntas. Esta escena es típica en la antigüedad: discípulo y maestro sentados para dialogar (Padilla, 2007). ¿Cómo analizar el texto bíblico para diseñar una clase que tenga pertinencia con la realidad del discípulo, que fomente un encuentro con Dios para dar luz y dirección en su realidad presente?

Dialoguemos con el texto, hagamos una lista de las preguntas de nuestro interés y las que podrían hacer los demás. Con mucha probabilidad ya tenemos algunas preguntas porque Dios está ministrando desde el primer día que hicimos la lectura bíblica. Es posible que el texto nos diga algo que nos abra el apetito (López, 2003). Usualmente preguntamos a la Biblia cosas que nos interesan en nuestra situación; son nuestras inquietudes, preguntas o problemas lo que determinan qué preguntas haremos a los textos. Tal vez nos llame la atención algunos versículos más que otros, lo

42. Este tipo de lectura enfocada en el lector es lo que se conoce como la teoría de la recepción o lector responsivo (López, 2003).

43. Lucas 10.39

cual es necesario que consideremos con cuidado. Jesús reconoció que su enseñanza no venía de él, por eso les dijo... *solamente digo lo que el Padre me ha enseñado.*[44] Esa también debe ser nuestra experiencia, enseñar lo que Dios quiere. Aunque usted desconozca lo que pasó, está pasando o pasará en la vida de quienes estarán sentados escuchándoles en clase, Dios sí lo sabe y tiene palabra que transforma para cada uno de nosotros. Nosotros seremos facilitadores para que tengan su propio encuentro con Dios.

Cuidémonos de deshumanizarnos. Nos molestamos,[45] nos cansamos del camino,[46] necesitamos retirarnos para estar solos,[47] nos enfrentamos a peligros que debemos huir,[48] lloramos,[49] sentimos angustia —en ocasiones, es tan terrible que sufrimos mucho y nos confundimos,[50] experimentamos el rechazo,[51] nos sentimos solos,[52] somos maltratados.[53] Según el Evangelio de Juan, nuestro Maestro experimentó también esta naturaleza humana, por lo cual nos entiende. También el apóstol Pablo nos recuerda el sufrimiento, la obediencia y la humildad de Jesús.[54] Dios no cancela nuestra humanidad, él nos conoce muy bien y sabe todo acerca de nosotros.[55] Somos personas inmersas en el proceso de santificación, llamados a santificar el nombre de Dios mediante nuestra

---

44. Juan 8.28b
45. Juan 2.15-216
46. Juan 4.6
47. Juan 6.15
48. Juan 8.59; 10.39; 12.36
49. Juan 11.35
50. Juan 12.27
51. Juan 12.48; 15.18
52. Juan 16.32
53. Juan 18.22; 19.1-3
54. Filipenses 2.8
55. Salmos 139.1-4

obediencia, así como Cristo lo hizo.[56] Con el privilegio de contar con su modelo de vida vencedor.

Dios nos manda que comamos del rollo primero, al igual que lo hizo con el profeta Ezequiel, y luego dar el mensaje.[57] Hagamos nuestra la enseñanza, disfrutemos ser alimentados y servidos por Dios. Durante este proceso de estudio Dios dará salud a nuestra alma y tendrá un trato personal, muy personal con nosotros. El escritor bíblico dice que la palabra de Dios es más cortante que cualquier espada de dos filos, y penetra hasta lo más profundo del alma y del espíritu, hasta lo más íntimo de la persona; y somete a juicio los pensamientos y las intenciones del corazón.[58] También, tiene el poder de sanar y renovarnos para ser instrumentos de Dios. El Salmista se preguntó: ¿Quién se da cuenta de sus propios errores? Entonces se dirigió a Dios y le dijo: ¡Perdona, Señor, mis faltas ocultas! Acto seguido le pidió que le quitara su orgullo y no permitiera que lo dominara.[59] En su encuentro con Dios y la palabra, el Salmista conciencia de la realidad de su fragilidad humana, de la necesidad de autoestudio y reflexión para identificar aquellos errores íntimos, y descubrir sus conflictos ocultos para superarlos. Contemplar a Dios le lleva a reconocer su poder y pedirle su ayuda para vivir con integridad (Pagán, 2007).

También tenemos que hacerle preguntas al texto que tengan relación con la realidad, las necesidades y los intereses de los discípulos. De esta manera nos preparamos para responder según la pertinencia y relevancia que identifiquemos en la participación. Por ejemplo, si enseñamos a un grupo de adulto, pensaremos en la vida de familia, el área profesional, la necesidad de empleo, de obtener una casa, el interés para una paternidad adecuada, una

56. Mateo 6.9; Filipenses 9.10-11

57. Ezequiel 3.1

58. Hebreos 4.12

59. Salmos 19.12-13

relación de pareja saludable. Además, ¿qué está pasando hoy en el mundo? Pensemos en el contexto del discípulo, la situación del país, la posible situación personal, la sociedad global, la situación política. También, en lo que pasó durante la semana, en lo que pasó ayer, en lo que se pronostica que pase después.

Entonces, el diálogo con el texto bíblico para su aplicación requiere una lectura consciente. Esto significa poner toda nuestra atención a lo que el texto nos dice; pensar y buscar para darnos cuenta en qué se relaciona con nuestra realidad, encontrándole su significado y utilidad personal. Por ejemplo, supongamos que la enseñanza es sobre confiar en el Señor y tenemos como base bíblica el Salmo 23. Es un salmo de confianza, donde se afirma la presencia y el cuidado de Dios; también, manifiesta la esperanza y la fortaleza (Pagán, 2007; González, 1998). Muchos lo saben de memoria y podrían ver la clase de manera trivial si no somos facilitadores para la conexión con su vida.

La actividad de aplicación es precedida por el estudio bíblico. El Salmo presenta dos imágenes poéticas que no son parte de nuestro contexto actual: la comparación de Dios con el pastor que atiende a sus ovejas (versículos 1-4); y la de Dios con el buen anfitrión que trata con atención expresiva y cariñosa a su invitado (versículos 5 y 6). Estas imágenes son el "detrás del texto" que tendrían que ser compartidas en clase para contestar las preguntas sobre su trasfondo histórico y social que nos ayudan a comprender lo que el texto pudo significar en su contexto inicial. Ahí también compartiremos que los Salmos son diálogos íntimos y profundos con Dios de personas como nosotros, en medio de las realidades cotidianas, donde se expresan los sentimientos más hondos tal y cuales son ("en del texto"). Luego, apliquemos sus declaraciones de fe en medio de las circunstancias reales que vivimos ("delante del texto").

Pensemos primero nosotros en el contexto de la realidad en que vivimos. Ubiquémonos en el momento histórico que tocó vivir en

Puerto Rico en septiembre de 2017, con la visita del huracán María que afectó a todo el país, siendo para todos una experiencia de pérdida en diversas maneras, tales como: seres queridos, propiedades, empleo, energía eléctrica, agua potable, alimentos, salud. Ciertamente las afirmaciones que el salmista expresa podrían llevarnos a pensar que lo motivó a escribirlas unas experiencias gratas de satisfacción espiritual y física. Vemos que culminó con una declaración de fe y seguridad, relacionó su futuro con Dios, además de encontrar bendiciones presentes para disfrutar. Pero, ¿qué tal si ese texto tuvo su origen en medio de una crisis de fe, de una situación de necesidad personal que lo llevó a reflexionar sobre lo que creía y determinó afirmar su fe? Si lo viéramos de esa manera, ¿encontraríamos que el Salmo 23 tiene alguna pertinencia a nuestra realidad actual?

Veamos en la Tabla 1 un ejemplo del ejercicio de aplicación. Usamos la estrategia de contraste para inferir cuál pudo ser la situación de necesidad del salmista, las circunstancias que vivía (columna B), a partir de sus declaraciones de fe (columna A).

Tabla 1: Contraste del Salmo 23

A Salmos 23*	B Necesidad de confianza en el Señor
Jehová es mi pastor; nada me faltará.	Necesito dirección; y muchas cosas más.
En lugares de delicados pastos me hará descansar; junto a aguas de reposo me pastoreará.	¿Cómo conseguiré mi alimento? ¿Cómo conseguiré mi paz?
Confortará mi alma; me guiará por sendas de justicia por amor de su nombre.	Estoy angustiado, mi vida está afectada, no veo justicia en lo que me está pasando.
Aunque ande en valle de sombra de muerte, no temeré mal alguno porque tú estarás conmigo.	Siento que me muero y veo que estoy solo en medio del peligro.
Tu vara y tu cayado me infundirán aliento.	Perdí el ánimo, ¿cómo regresará?
Aderezas mesa delante de mí en presencia de mis angustiadores.	Pienso en los que estarán murmurando de mí y también me duele.
Unges mi cabeza con aceite; mi copa está rebosando. Ciertamente el bien y la misericordia me seguirán todos los días de mi vida, y en la casa de Jehová moraré por largos días.	Veo como me encuentro, la estrechez que atravieso. Veo el mal que me sigue y siento la ausencia de tu amor; te siento lejos de mí, sin esperanza y sin tu protección.

*Versión Reina-Valera 1960

La estrategia de contraste en el diálogo con el Salmo 23, nos lleva a reflexionar sobre la declaración de fe del salmista aún en medio de la crisis. Nos invita a pensar en lo que creemos y a tomar una determinación sobre cuál será nuestra actitud ante la vida. Las personas tienen experiencias humanas que afectan su vida de manera adversa, no importa cuál sea su fe. Esto incluye al que es miembro de la iglesia y al que nos visita. Estas experiencias no están lejos de las que tuvo el pueblo de Israel y la iglesia cristiana primitiva. En el Antiguo y Nuevo Testamento encontramos relatos sobre la vida cotidiana de un pueblo, su experiencia religiosa y los resultados de sus acciones. La Biblia sigue siendo útil para ver el significado de la vida hoy y para darnos un reto nuevo cada día. Aquí encontramos la razón para ganar el interés y la atención del joven y adulto a la enseñanza bíblica; sea creyente o no, sea miembro o visita, la enseñanza de la Biblia es para todos. Tengamos primero la experiencia de completar la dinámica que daremos a los discípulos. Además de Dios ministrarnos primero, tendremos la oportunidad de validar la dinámica, hacerle los arreglos para asegurar su comprensión y su articulación con el propósito de la clase. Esto es parte de su preparación. Es decir, entre a su lugar de estudio privado, cierre la puerta y siéntese con Dios para hacer la actividad preparada. Esta dinámica de interacción, de tocar piso con su realidad, será su plataforma para comprender la enseñanza. Es entonces y solo luego de experimentar un encuentro interactivo con Dios, entre el Maestro y nosotros como sus humildes discípulos, que guiaremos en clase a que tengan el suyo propio, a profundizar aún más en su fe. Así podremos decir como el apóstol Pablo: lo que aprendisteis y recibisteis y oísteis y visteis en mí, esto haced.[60]

El aprendizaje en el sentido bíblico convoca a la persona del discípulo para responder a la palabra de Dios con un compromiso

60. Filipenses 4.9

personal y comunitario, lo que nos llevará a otro nivel, a la acción. El resultado deseado de la educación cristiana siempre será su propósito, que la totalidad de la vida del discípulo, de la iglesia, sea transformada con la ayuda del Espíritu Santo para participar en la construcción del reino de Dios iniciado por Jesucristo aquí en la tierra.

REPASO

El repaso debe ser el día antes de la clase, no más lejos de eso. Durante todo el proceso de nuestra semana de estudio estaremos también preparando nuestra guía para la clase. De manera que al final de nuestro estudio tendremos la guía de clase completada; solo tendremos que editar, hacer algunas pocas modificaciones si fuera necesario, revisar nuestras notas, orar por cada uno y por la dirección del Espíritu Santo en la presentación. Veremos un formato de la guía de la clase, la cual describimos en el próximo paso, Planificación.

2

PLANIFICACIÓN

"Como buenos administradores de los diferentes dones de Dios, cada uno de ustedes sirva a los demás según lo que haya recibido".

I PEDRO 4.10

La segunda **P** es nuestra organización estratégica, consciente de lo que servimos; es cuando preparamos una clase con la creatividad requerida que despierte el interés de escuchar, mantener la atención, propiciar la participación, facilitar la comprensión y promover la acción de los discípulos en respuesta al mensaje recibido.

Lo que este paso implica podríamos relacionarlo con la narración de Génesis cuando Dios plantó el jardín de Edén y puso al hombre en el jardín para que lo cultivara y lo cuidara.[1] Cuenta el escritor que Dios hizo crecer toda clase de árboles hermosos que daban fruto bueno para comer. Además, que de Edén nacía un río que regaba el jardín y que de allí se dividía en otras áreas.[2] Parecía que el jardín tenía todo, estaba completo. Entonces, cabe la pregunta si era necesaria la tarea de cultivar y cuidar el jardín. ¿A quién más necesitaba el huerto si tenía a su Dios Creador quien pensó en cada detalle? Con solo decir la orden, el Todopoderoso

1. Génesis 2.15
2. Génesis 2.8-10

pudo hacer que fuera auto-cultivado y auto-cuidado. Sin embargo, Dios decidió delegar la responsabilidad de cultivar y cuidar el jardín. Ciertamente Dios nos dio una tarea a realizar; algo que es necesario para que se cumpla el propósito divino.[3]

La planificación trata de mayordomía, de la buena administración del don de Dios, de cumplir bien la tarea educativa que Dios nos delegó. Sabemos que el alcance de dicha tarea dependerá de la comprensión de su llamado, lo que compartimos antes en la preparación. Como servidores somos llamados a cumplir la tarea de edificar el cuerpo de Cristo, de ser guía y modelo de vida para que otros entiendan la fe en Jesucristo. Ciertamente el Espíritu es quien produce la fe.[4] Sin embargo, a nosotros nos toca vivirla. El Dr. Justo L. González nos dice en su libro Conoce tu fe, que esto no quiere decir que la mente y el entendimiento no tengan lugar en la vida de fe; más bien, la fe nos lleva a emplear nuestra mente para entender a Dios, la verdad de su amor y su voluntad para con nosotros (González, 2017).

Desde el Antiguo Testamento Dios manda que le amemos con toda nuestra mente; además de con todo lo que somos, la vida misma, y todas nuestras fuerzas. Este mandamiento de Dios es la profesión de fe tradicional para el pueblo de Israel, conocida como Shemá (por su primera palabra: Oye, escucha).[5] En el Antiguo Testamento el corazón simbolizaba la mente, el pensamiento, la inteligencia, el entendimiento, la meditación; esto es similar a lo que hoy decimos "el cerebro" (González, 1998). También en el Nuevo Testamento el Señor Jesús enseñó que del corazón del hombre proceden los malos pensamientos y toda forma de maldad.[6] Según el Evangelio de Marcos, el Maestro dio mucha im-

3. En Génesis 1.27-28 Dios asigna la misma responsabilidad a la primera pareja humana.
4. Gálatas 5.22
5. Deuteronomio 6.4-5.
6. Marcos 7.21

portancia a que los discípulos entendieran y comprendieran su fe (Marcos 4.40-41; 6.50-52; 7.18; 8.17-18; 9.31-32; 16.14).

Entonces, es necesario que entendamos lo que Dios quiere que hagamos porque la palabra de Dios es para vivirla. Entender es tener una idea clara de las cosas, conocer, saber. Jesús dio importancia al entendimiento de su enseñanza, a que ésta estuviera clara porque requería responder a su demanda, la toma de decisiones para la acción.[7] Por ejemplo, luego de enseñar sobre el valor del Reino por medio de parábolas, preguntó: ¿Habéis entendido todas estas cosas? Otro ejemplo es la historia de Felipe y el etíope. El Espíritu dijo a Felipe que se acercara donde se encontraba el etíope. Acudiendo Felipe, le oyó que leía al profeta Isaías y le preguntó: ¿Entiendes lo que lees? Y el etíope respondió: ¿Cómo podré si alguno no me enseñare?[8]

Dios es nuestro modelo a seguir. La Biblia nos enseña que nuestro Dios es de orden, quien toma su tiempo para pensar bien lo que quiere hacer y cuál es su propósito antes de actuar; además, quien hace planes. Por ejemplo, pensó crear a la humanidad y dijo: hagamos al hombre a nuestra imagen. El tendrá poder sobre los peces, las aves, los animales domésticos y los salvajes y sobre los que se arrastran por el suelo. Luego el relato bíblico dice que cuando Dios creó al hombre, lo creó a su imagen; varón y mujer los creó, y les dio su bendición: tengan muchos, muchos hijos; llenen el mundo y gobiérnenlo; dominen a los peces y a las aves, y a todos los animales que se arrastran.[9] Entonces, según lo pensó así lo hizo. También la Biblia nos presenta a un Dios que hace planes: Yo sé los planes que tengo para ustedes, planes para su bienestar y no para su mal, a fin de darles un futuro lleno de esperanza.[10]

---

7. Mateo 13.51.
8. Hechos 8.30-31
9. Génesis 1.26-28
10. Jeremías 29.11

Por tanto, aunque tengamos como recurso la revista bíblica, el expositor u otra guía de estudio, hagamos nuestro plan. Un tema que fue elaborado pensando en toda la comunidad de fe requiere ser estudiado y realizar aquello que sea necesario para enfocar la enseñanza, por ejemplo: tomar cuenta las particulares del grupo, su contexto comunitario y el mensaje de nuestro Dios, quien es personal. Entonces nuestra tarea incluye descubrir las necesidades espirituales de los discípulos para ser pertinentes, utilizar ejemplos con los que se puedan relacionar los discípulos porque representen su realidad de vida, y escuchar la voz del Espíritu Santo que se manifiesta en diferentes maneras.

Ahora bien, la planificación de la clase va a corresponder a lo que pensamos o entendemos sobre lo que es una clase. Por lo tanto, hablemos primero del concepto de clase y, luego, sobre el plan para llevarla a cabo. De esta manera estaremos todos en la misma página. Esto es necesario porque no usamos como referencia una preparación académica para la práctica docente. Principalmente esto significa dos cosas. En primer lugar, que nuestro llamado a enseñar tiene correspondencia con el don de Dios. En segundo lugar, que tenemos una responsabilidad de formarnos y cultivarnos para aprender a usar el don de Dios, dirigidos a cumplir con la edificación del cuerpo de Cristo. Es decir, el don proviene de Dios y a nosotros nos toca ser buenos administradores.

EL CONCEPTO DE LA CLASE

Ciertamente la práctica educativa del Maestro contribuye a nuestro entendimiento sobre lo que es una clase. El Dr. Samuel Pagán comparte en su libro Jesús de Nazaret: vida, enseñanza y significado, que las dinámicas educativas que se llevaban a efecto en el primer siglo contribuyeron en la personalidad del Maestro

(Pagán, 2012). Explica que los procesos educativos no eran estáticos, sino dinámicos y renovadores; su estrategia incluía el diálogo, la observación, el análisis, la reflexión personal y colectiva, así como la evaluación crítica y sobria de la vida y la existencia humana.

Aunque los evangelios canónicos no indican de forma específica que Jesús haya asistido a una escuela oficial o formal, su estilo de enseñanza demuestra que recibió un buen modelo. La historia bíblica que narra cuando de niño se quedó en Jerusalén sin que sus padres se dieran cuenta y lo encontraron sentado entre los maestros de la ley, escuchándolos y haciéndoles preguntas, evidencia que el Señor desarrolló su estilo educativo temprano en su vida.[11] Ciertamente fueron diversos los factores que contribuyeron de forma significativa en su vida: el contexto íntimo de su familia, las dinámicas sociales de su comunidad y su entorno laboral en Galilea. Además, los programas educativos a los que se expuso en las sinagogas que frecuentaba y sus diálogos con los diversos líderes religiosos del judaísmo (Pagán, 2019). Nuestro Maestro no estuvo enajenado del contexto geográfico, social, económico, político, religioso y espiritual que le rodeaba.

Consideremos la tendencia actual sobre la educación declarada por la UNESCO. Esta es la única organización de las Naciones Unidas que dispone de un mandato para abarcar todos los aspectos de la educación, a quien se le asignó la función de liderar y coordinar la Agenda de Educación Mundial 2030.[12] La UNESCO manifiesta que la educación debe estar centrado en el aprendizaje activo, contextualizado, transferible y autónomo, con prácticas pedagógicas inclusivas y transformadoras, que

11. Lucas 2.41-52

12. La UNESCO, United Nations Educational, Scientific and Cultural Organization (Organización de las Naciones Unidas para la Educación, la Ciencia y la Cultura) es un organismo de la ONU que fue fundado en 1945 y que tiene su sede en París (Francia).

consideren vínculos con las dimensiones de la vida, maximicen el uso de las tecnologías de la información y de la comunicación (TIC), e incluyan temas relevantes de la sociedad global, interconectada, digital y dinámica. Esto sobre la base filosófica que es un derecho humano para todos, a lo largo de toda la vida, y que el acceso a la enseñanza debe ir acompañado de la calidad.

Según la nueva visión de la UNESCO, la educación de calidad fomenta la creatividad y el conocimiento.[13] Además, garantiza la adquisición de aptitudes analíticas, de solución de problemas y otras habilidades cognitivas, interpersonales y sociales de alto nivel. También, propicia el desarrollo de las competencias, los valores y las actitudes que permiten a los ciudadanos llevar vidas saludables y plenas, tomar decisiones con conocimiento de causa y responder a los desafíos. Ciertamente la declaración de la UNESCO es una referencia para la educación cristiana en cuanto a las dinámicas educativas de nuestro contexto.

La definición de la UNESCO para una educación de calidad (creatividad y conocimiento) es correspondiente a la práctica educativa de nuestro Maestro, Jesús de Nazaret. El Maestro enseñó de forma efectiva en la sociedad judía, pues consideró las dinámicas educativas de su entorno para lograr el efecto que deseaba (Pagán, 2019). Por ejemplo, en la sociedad de su época no eran comunes las actividades de leer y escribir. Jesús demostró su creatividad en el uso de una estrategia viable que incluyó una diversidad de facilitadores para la comprensión de su mensaje, tales como el drama, la exageración, el humor, la imaginación, la reiteración. Mantenía atenta a su audiencia y propiciaba el diálogo a sus enseñanzas, haciendo uso de los recursos que tenía a su disposición. Aprovechó las interacciones que se ponían de manifiesto en el contexto que vivía, las cuales le brindaron la información,

---

13. Declaración de Incheon y Marco de Acción. Incheon (República de Corea) 21 de mayo de 2015. https://unesdoc.unesco.org/ark:/48223/pf0000245656_spa

el trasfondo, la formación, los valores, el estilo, las prioridades, el contenido, las comprensiones de la vida y la existencia humana. El pueblo reconocía su gran capacidad comunicativa, su gran imaginación y creatividad al articular sus enseñanzas con un estilo que se daba a entender. El lenguaje que utilizaba era a menudo común y popular, con el que la comunidad judía podía relacionarse sin dificultad. Aunque no era el único maestro de la época, se distinguía por su creatividad, contenido y la cantidad de sus ejemplos (Pagán, 2012).

La clase bíblica es parte de nuestro culto a Dios, donde reconocemos su presencia y somos moldeados por él (González, 2017). Es un encuentro interactivo entre quien enseña y los discípulos; entre los discípulos; y entre el Espíritu Santo y la persona. Todos somos personas, todos somos discípulos. Todos vivimos en el mismo mundo que experimenta transformaciones sociales, culturales y tecnológicas.[14] Estas transformaciones también moldean a la persona y dirigen a nuevas tendencias en la manera de enseñar, en la dinámica educativa a practicar. Dichas transformaciones requieren que revisemos nuestro estilo de ofrecer la clase para corresponder a la realidad contextual (pertinente) y ser creativo en el uso de una estrategia que dirija a la comprensión del significado para su vida (relevante), de tal manera que se comprometan con su aprendizaje y lo practiquen.

La tendencia actual sobre la educación declarada por la UNESCO es una referencia para revisar si lo que pensamos o entendemos sobre lo que es una clase tiene relación a la realidad en que vivimos. Las contribuciones de la UNESCO sobre el estilo de enseñanza que corresponde practicar hoy día, deben ser aprovechadas por la iglesia porque nos orienta cómo entiende y aprende

14. Declaración de Buenos Aires - E2030: Educación y habilidades para el siglo 21. Reunión Regional de Ministros de Educación de América Latina y el Caribe24-25 de enero de 2017, Buenos Aires, República Argentina. https://unesdoc.unesco.org/ark:/48223/pf0000247286

la persona del mismo mundo al que servimos. Tan importante es que tengamos claro cuál es la enseñanza que compartiremos, como conocer cuál es la manera más efectiva para que se entienda lo que enseñamos y que la pongamos en práctica. Jesús aprovechó las dinámicas educativas formales y curriculares que aprendió en la sinagoga; hizo uso de los recursos retóricos que tenía a su disposición, fue creativo en el uso del género parabólico que ya existía, dándole su toque particular para que el pueblo pudiera entender y apreciar su enseñanza. Así también, los primeros misioneros usaron muy bien la infraestructura de comunicación y los caminos del imperio romano en el desempeño de sus funciones educativas y evangelísticas (Pagán, 2019).

También, es importante señalar que la educación es conocida por dos nombres, dependiendo el nivel o las edades de su grupo: Pedagogía o Andragogía. La Pedagogía es la ciencia que se ocupa especialmente a la educación de los niños, aunque también el término se utiliza de manera general para identificar la capacidad de enseñar o educar. La educación de adultos es conocida como la Andragogía. Las historias de vida del ser humano, especialmente el adulto, son diferentes y tienen sus propias particularidades, tanto en la vida personal y laboral, en conocimientos y capacidades (Castilla, 2018). Entonces, este estilo inclusivo propiciará mayor participación. El norteamericano Malcolm Shepherd Knowles (1913-1997), denominado como el padre de la Andragogía, identificó un conjunto de principios fundamentales a considerarse en la enseñanza a los adultos, los cuales la distinguen de la enseñanza a los niños (Castillo, 2018):

1. El adulto necesita saber por qué tiene que aprender algo antes de someterse al proceso de aprendizaje

Como un adulto es partícipe de su formación, debe identificar claramente la necesidad de su aprendizaje.

2. El autoconcepto

Por ser una persona con un grado de madurez tal que le permite saber que tiene la responsabilidad de su crecimiento y de su vida, es quien decide si participa en un proceso de aprendizaje.

3. El papel de la experiencia de los participantes

Esta persona trae un cúmulo de conocimientos generales (de su vida, de su o sus grados académicos, y de otras tantas fuentes de información), así como las experiencias acumuladas por el tiempo y eventos vividos.

4. Disposición de aprender del participante

Los temas de enseñanza deberán ser significativos al adulto para que los relacione con su vida o algún rol de ella.

5. Orientación hacia el aprendizaje

Es conveniente considerar dos cosas: (a) que proponga obtener conocimientos, destrezas, valores y actitudes de una manera eficaz al presentárselo en un contexto de aplicación a las situaciones de la vida real, y (b) que el tiempo sea el apropiado en la formación.

6. Motivación para aprender

Es la generación del desplazamiento de una actitud hacia otra distinta, la fuente de la motivación viene del individuo mismo.

En el salón de clase tenemos la representación de la sociedad. Esto es una paráfrasis de lo que dijo el filósofo, psicólogo y educador estadounidense John Dewey (1859-1952), figura reconocida de la primera mitad del siglo 20. Dewey entendía que la escuela es el microcosmo de la sociedad. Tras dedicar mucho tiempo a observar el crecimiento de sus propios hijos, Dewey estaba convencido de que no había ninguna diferencia en la dinámica de la experiencia de niños y adultos. Unos y otros son seres activos que aprenden mediante su enfrentamiento con situaciones problemáticas que surgen en el curso de las actividades que han merecido su interés. Según Dewey, un maestro de esa índole tiene que poder ver el mundo con los ojos de niño y con los del adulto.

Dewey admitió que la mayoría de los maestros no poseen los conocimientos teóricos y prácticos que son necesarios para enseñar de esta manera, pero consideraba que podían aprender a hacerlo. Este educador hizo énfasis en la participación activa de los estudiantes en la sala de clase y la práctica del aprendizaje, a través de la experiencia y de la reflexión crítica. Desarrolló una filosofía que abogaba por la unidad entre la teoría y la práctica.[15]

Dewey reconocía que pedía mucho a los maestros y por ello, al describir su función e importancia social a finales del decenio de 1890, volvió a recurrir al evangelismo social, que había abandonado, llamando al maestro "el anunciador del verdadero reino de Dios." La aportación de Dewey a la educación también corresponde a la tendencia actual de la educación. Sus recomendaciones sobre la participación activa de los estudiantes, la oportunidad de practicar lo aprendido a través de la experiencia y de la reflexión crítica siguen siendo pertinentes en el siglo 21.

También es importante concienciar sobre las distintas generaciones que representan nuestra sociedad y sus características, que corresponden al contexto en que vivimos. Puesto que a los sucesos históricos, sociales y culturales causan gran influencia en la manera de pensar, y los principios que rigen sus actuaciones. De acuerdo con la definición del Pew Research Center, son cinco generaciones (Alvarado, 2019):

---

15. Perspectivas: revista trimestral de educación comparada (París, UNESCO: Oficina Internacional de Educación), vol. XXIII, nos 1-2, 1993, págs. 289-305.

- **Generación Z.** Nacidos entre 1997 y 2012. Tienen entre 7 y 22 años. Se les llama Centennials. Esta generación está marcada por un cambio de siglo y un cambio de milenio. Los jóvenes pertenecientes a esta generación están ingresando a las universidades y han crecido en un mundo gobernado por la tecnología. Están acostumbrados a una conexión permanente a la Internet como parte de sus vidas cotidianas, lo que ha provocado que tengan escasas habilidades sociales, aunque valoran la diversidad. Es la primera generación formada en los nuevos avances tecnológicos, rodeados de ordenadores, vídeos y videojuegos, música digital, telefonía móvil y otros entretenimientos y herramientas afines.
- **Generación Y.** Naciones entre 1981 y 1996. Tienen entre 23 y 38 años. Se les llama Millennials. Es considerada como la última generación del siglo pasado, formada bajo la era de la informática. Suelen ser impacientes, insensibles y les molesta los estereotipos sobre todo el tener que seguir a una figura adulta y de autoridad. Conocidos también como los NETs, esta generación le da gran valor a su independencia y a la variedad que les ofrece el mundo actual. Esta población no se siente atraída por el sistema escolar porque no genera satisfacciones inmediatas.
- **Generación X.** Naciones entre 1965 y 1980. Tienen entre 39 y 54 años. Tiene un concepto de la vida en donde los deberes y responsabilidades se comparten entre el hombre y la mujer. Esta población dejó de ser una con esquemas tradicionales y rígidos para convertirse en una más flexible y abierta a los cambios presentando una diversidad de ideales. La diversidad de ideales incluye la equidad e igualdad de los derechos civiles entre todas las razas y géneros.

- **Baby Boomers.** Nacidos entre 1946 y 1964. Tienen entre 55 y 73 años. Vio el nacimiento de los medios de comunicación audiovisuales, tales como la televisión y el cine. La integración del teléfono, así como los vuelos comerciales aceleraron los intercambios comunicativos entre las personas de esta generación. La creación y desarrollo del periódico, la radio, la televisión, el cine y teléfono causó un impacto directo en la forma de convivencia de las personas y en la manera en que se capacitaban y aprendían.
- **Generación S / Silente.** Nacidos entre 1928 y 1945. Tienen entre 74 y 91 años. Fue marcada directamente por los efectos y consecuencias de la Primera y Segunda Guerra Mundial. La creación del periódico, la radiofonía y los medios postales constituían los elementos de comunicación para la Generación S.

Además, una clase puede ser entendida por sus componentes esenciales para desarrollar un plan educativo efectivo.[16] La Figura 3 presenta los Componentes Esenciales del Plan Educativo Transformador. Son esenciales porque todos realizan una tarea muy importante para ejecutar la tarea educativa y están interrelacionados. Es un plan educativo porque existe una estructura cuidadosamente organizada que guía su práctica educativa. En el contexto de la educación cristiana, el concepto transformador tiene que ver con su propósito de educar para la transformación

16. En la década de los 90's se realizaron varios estudios con profesores universitarios en diferentes instituciones postsecundarias en los Estados Unidos. El propósito del estudio fue conocer cuáles eran sus esfuerzos para lograr desarrollar un plan educativo efectivo. Ellos describieron su marco de trabajo con los siguientes ocho componentes: propósito, contenido, secuencia, aprendiz, recursos instruccionales, procesos instruccionales, evaluación y ajuste. (Stark y Lattuca, 1997). El Espíritu Santo es la ayuda esencial, quien participa en todo el proceso (Nales, 2006).

de la persona del discípulo.[17] Esta transformación explica el cambio a una naturaleza nueva, creada a imagen de Dios, que afecta a la persona de manera integral y se refleja en todas sus relaciones (Nales, 2006).

La Figura 3 presenta los componentes esenciales de una práctica educativa para lograr la interacción, el compromiso y la acción. El modelo demuestra que el proceso interactivo consistirá en la estrategia que utilicemos.

Figura 3: Componentes Esenciales del Plan Educativo Transformador

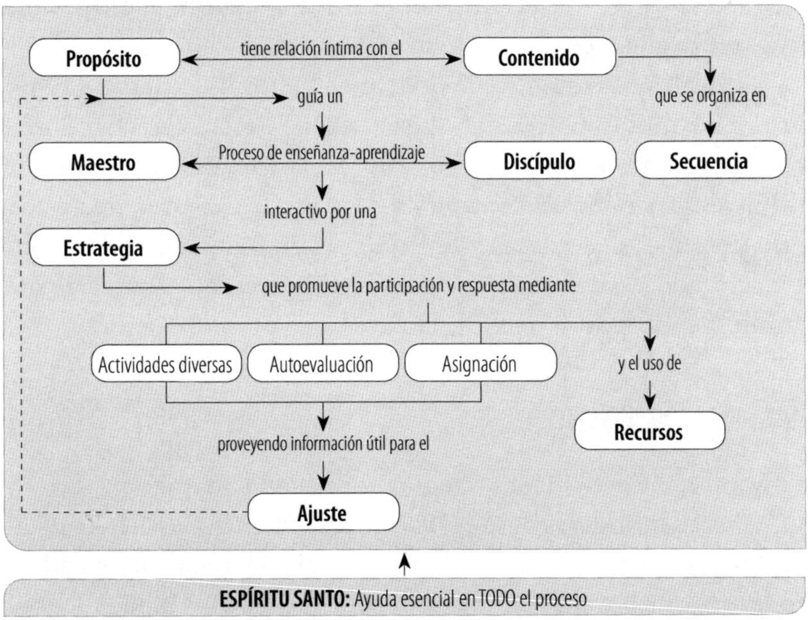

La estrategia es la respuesta a nuestra pregunta ¿Cómo lo voy a hacer? La importancia asignada a la estrategia para una práctica educativa que promueve la interacción, el compromiso y la acción, requiere que hagamos un alto para su descripción.

17. 1 Corintios 15.51-52; 2 Corintios 3.18; Romanos 12.2; Gálatas 4.19; 1 Tesalonicenses 5.23

ESTRATEGIA

La estrategia es un concepto de origen militar que luego fue aplicado a la educación.[18] Se dice que durante la Segunda Guerra Mundial un general tenía la habilidad de sentarse a la mesa y planificar en detalle toda una gigantesca operación: cuántos soldados, aviones, tanques, barcos, municiones, alimentos, combustibles, apoyo y logística necesitarían. Además, incluía elementos nuevos como opciones por si algunos fallaran en realizarse. Dichos elementos nuevos ofrecían flexibilidad a la planificación, lo que caracteriza el concepto de estrategia.

La Real Academia Española define el término estrategia como arte para dirigir un asunto. La enseñanza es reconocida como ciencia y como arte (Marzano, 2007). La llaman ciencia porque las investigaciones proveen guías para una enseñanza efectiva; y, arte porque quien enseña tiene que determinar cuál será la combinación de las actividades que funcionarán como estrategia para cumplir el propósito de la enseñanza.

ACTIVIDADES DIVERSAS

El nombre de actividades diversas corresponde a que son varias y distintas, distribuidas desde el inicio hasta el final de la clase. Estas actividades procuran señalar la pertinencia del tema (actividad de motivación); propiciar el diálogo sobre el estudio bíblico (actividad de estudio bíblico), vincular la enseñanza con la vida cotidiana (actividad de aplicación), dirigir al discípulo a reflexionar sobre su situación actual (autoevaluación), y practicar la enseñanza (asignación) en respuesta al llamado de Dios. La autoevaluación y la asignación son identificadas por separados para recordar que se lleve a cabo en cada clase.

18. Ortiz, Ángel L., 2003.

También podemos añadir mayor diversidad al proceso para facilitar la comprensión de lo que se enseña y promover mayor interacción, cuando consideramos lo que dice la Teoría de las Inteligencias Múltiples (Gardner, 2017). Ésta establece que la mente tiene la capacidad de tratar distintos tipos de contenidos, mostrar distintas competencias o inteligencias que dan lugar a diversas formas de enseñanza, en lugar de solo una. Afirma que cualquier limitación considerable de la mente puede modificarse, de tal modo que creemos más probabilidades para aprender. Aquí la inteligencia no significa la idea clásica de una capacidad general que todo ser humano posee en mayor o menor medida y que puede medirse mediante instrumentos estándar. Las inteligencias múltiples se refieren a las habilidades que valoran las culturas humanas, las facultades o competencias intelectuales humanas.

La idea de las inteligencias múltiples es muy antigua; sin embargo, fue revivida por el Dr. Howard Gardner en 1983 en su obra Estructuras de la mente. Su estudio respondió al pedido de la Fundación Bernard van Leer, con objeto de apoyar innovaciones útiles en la educación para beneficiar a los inválidos. En 1979 dicha Fundación pidió a la Escuela de Educación para Posgraduados de Harvard, que evaluara el estado del conocimiento científico referente al potencial humano y su logro. También, que resumiera los resultados de forma que ayudara al plan de acción y práctica educacionales en todo el mundo (Gardner, 2017).

El Dr. Gardner señaló la necesidad de una mejor clasificación de las competencias intelectuales humanas ante el producto de la investigación científica, de observaciones transculturales y del estudio educacional. Afirmó que todos los individuos son inteligentes de diferentes maneras porque poseen diversas competencias que funcionan juntas —aunque unas desarrolladas más que otras— y que pueden continuar su desarrollo a lo largo de la vida. Inicialmente nombró siete tipos de inteligencia: lingüística, lógico-matemática, musical, espacial, corporal, y dos formas de inteligencia personal: intrapersonal, que apunta hacia la propia persona, y la otra interpersonal, que se dirige hacia los demás. Explicó que en circunstancias ordinarias no se puede desarrollar ninguna de las dos formas de inteligencia sin la otra. Por lo tanto, describir cada forma como una inteligencia por separado sería una duplicación innecesaria igual que una separación artificial.

En el prólogo a la edición del décimo aniversario de su Teoría, el Dr. Gardner expresó que aunque decidió no alterar, por ahora, la lista original, sigue considerando que pueda existir alguna forma de inteligencia espiritual (Gardner, 2017). Sin embargo, más tarde declaró que los aspectos de la espiritualidad que tienen que ver con la experiencia fenomenológica o con los valores o comportamientos deseados se consideran mejor externos a la esfera intelectual. Entonces, debido a los criterios científicos vio más viable la sugerencia de una inteligencia existencial y aún merecen una mayor investigación (Gardner, 2000). En escritos más recientes, el Dr. Gardner añadió la inteligencia naturalista (Gardner, 2006).

Alguien dijo que la rueda ya fue inventada. Y como dice el Dr. Samuel Pagán, si los primeros cristianos usaron los caminos construidos para la guerra y llevaron el evangelio de la paz a todos los rincones del Imperio Romanos, aprovechemos la contribución de las ciencias para el servicio de nuestras funciones educativas y evangélicas (Pagán, 2019). Añada mayor diversidad en la misma clase si utiliza competencias diferentes en la secuencia de las actividades; entre clases, si cuando planifica la clase asegura que las actividades usen competencias diferentes de las usadas en la clase anterior. Tengamos presente la interacción productiva de las competencias humanas, por lo que una actividad podría incluir varias de ellas. Sin embargo, podemos evitar que la clase sea predecible al no repetir la misma actividad o el mismo uso de las competencias.

Entonces, hagamos nuestra parte en practicar una buena administración del don; el Espíritu Santo hará la suya.

Ahora veamos una breve descripción de las inteligencias múltiples, bajo el nombre de competencias; así evitamos relacionarla con la suposición clásica de la inteligencia. Integramos algunos ejemplos de actividades para demostrar cómo se puede usar en clase. Sin intención de ignorar la relación íntima entre las competencias personales explicadas por el Dr. Gardner, identificamos la intrapersonal e interpersonal por separado para facilitar el nombrar los ejemplos de las actividades de cada una.

Competencia lingüística

¿Qué es? Es la competencia del lenguaje; la sensibilidad para el significado de las palabras (semántica), de sus sonidos (fonología); para las diferentes funciones del lenguaje (pragmática), y la capacidad para observar las reglas que gobiernan el orden (sintaxis) de las palabras. Esta sensibilidad aguda se ve en acción en un poeta. Sin embargo, esta competencia es compartida en toda la especie humana y la mayoría de nosotros poseemos la misma en grado significativo aunque no seamos poetas. El desarrollo de las habilidades lingüísticas en el ser humano se ve en los primeros meses de vida, cuando emiten sonidos; ya al segundo año de vida expresa palabras claves y frases significativas; al tercer año expresa mayor secuencia de mayor complejidad; aumentando notablemente su fluidez a los cuatro y cinco años, en formas que se parecen mucho a la sintaxis del adulto. El lenguaje es el medio óptimo para comunicarnos; puede ser transmitido por medio del gesto y la escritura, pero en esencia sigue siendo producto del tracto vocal y un mensaje para el oído humano. Sin embargo, hay una diversidad de formas en que los humanos, hábiles o con impedimentos de esta competencia en alguna manera, nos comunicamos. *¿Cómo la integramos a la clase?*

1. Lectura.
   Lectura del pasaje bíblico de manera individual, en silencio. Añádale que hagan una marca al versículo que le llame la atención. Lectura alternada; por ejemplo, los hombres leen un versículo y las mujeres otro o la maestra lee una porción y la clase lee otra. Lectura al unísono: todos juntos.

2. Escritura.
   Pida que escriba un salmo de su propia inspiración expresando su realidad actual. Escoge entre las clasificaciones de los salmos: himnos de alabanza a Dios; lamentos (súplicas y sufrimiento); acciones de gracias por la ayuda recibida.

3. Narración de una historia.
   En lugar de leer algún pasaje bíblico largo, pida que un voluntario/a narre la historia para el grupo. Por ejemplo, la historia de José, hijo de Jacob; la parábola del buen samaritano.

4. Definición de términos.
   Pregunte por sinónimos y antónimos. Busque en la aplicación de la Real Academia Española. Identifique la etimología de la palabra.
   Pida que subraye aquellas palabras que no conoce su significado.
   Entregue un palaberinto con el significado del vocabulario de la historia para que los discípulos lo identifiquen.

5. Presentar una parte de un refrán popular que tenga relación con el tema para que lo completen y compartan

su significado. Esa relación lo llevará a compartir el propósito.

6. Identificar la función del idioma en el texto. Pregunte ¿Cómo lo dijo? Explique que se refiere a identificar la función del lenguaje que refleje la intención comunicativa del escritor. Por ejemplo:
   - informativo (acto comunicativo= referencial);
   - expresiva (exclamativas, opinión=emotiva);
   - imperativa (exhortativa, interrogativa que indique una orden, un pedido=apelativa);
   - relacional (verifica que el canal de comunicación funcione correctamente=fática) ¿Ok "Claro" "¿Sabes?"
   - estética (expresa sentimiento, refranes-poética)
   - definición (metalingüística)

7. Torbellino de ideas.
   Anime a ofrecer cualesquiera ideas que se le ocurran sin importar si las ideas parecen razonables o correctas. Escriba en la pizarra ideas en respuesta a alguna pregunta o situación. No se permite ninguna crítica hasta después de que todos han contribuido con sus ideas. Las ideas son registradas para su evaluación posterior.

8. Reacción escrita inmediata (REI).
   En cualquier momento durante la clase, el discípulo responde en forma escrita y corta a un estímulo presentado por el maestro, con el propósito de animar a expresar su reacción o comprensión de algún concepto o tema. Hay una variedad de formatos para utilizar esta técnica. Entre el más usual está el formular un pensamiento incompleto para ser completado.

9. Lista focalizada.
   Enfoca la atención de los discípulos en un solo término, nombre o concepto de una lección particular y los dirige a hacer una lista de algunas ideas que están íntimamente relacionadas con el punto focal seleccionado. Esta técnica se utiliza para explorar el conocimiento que tiene el discípulo de un tema.

10. Parafraseo directo.
    Pida que digan en sus propias palabras la definición de un término, concepto o el texto clave de la clase.

11. Mencione alguna noticia del momento si está relacionada al tema, y articule con el propósito de la clase.

12. Comparta alguna anécdota histórica, que leyó en un libro u otra que se relacione con el tema y lo lleve a presentar el propósito.

13. Tirillas cómicas.
    Entregue una tirilla cómica con los espacios para escribir un diálogo que conecte el mensaje con su realidad de vida.

Competencia musical

¿Qué es? Es la competencia para percibir, distinguir, transformar e interpretar formas musicales. Los principales elementos de esta capacidad son la sensibilidad a la melodía o al tono, y el ritmo o los sonidos. Luego le sigue el timbre, como las cualidades características de un tono. Esto plantea que el sentido auditivo es esencial para toda participación musical; aunque un aspecto de la experiencia musical, la organización rítmica, puede existir aparte

de toda realización auditiva, siendo también accesible a los individuos que no pueden apreciar sus aspectos auditivos. Se dice que de todos los dones con que se pueden estar dotados los individuos, ninguno surge más temprano que el talento musical. Durante la infancia, los niños normales cantan y por igual balbucean: pueden emitir sonidos únicos, producir patrones ondulantes e incluso emitir sonidos únicos, producir patrones ondulantes, e incluso imitar patrones y tonos prosódicos cantados por otros. Sin embargo, el logro musical no es un reflejo estricto de la habilidad innata, sino que puede derivarse del estímulo y adiestramiento culturales. Existen íntimos lazos entre la música y el lenguaje corporal o de gestos. Por ejemplo, los niños pequeños relacionan de manera natural la música con el movimiento del cuerpo, haciéndosele imposible cantar sin que al mismo tiempo mantengan alguna actividad física que acompañe el canto. *¿Cómo la integramos a la clase?*

1. Escuche una canción.
   Use una grabación.
   Pida que alguien la cante en vivo.
   Invite a la congregación a cantar una porción de un himno o un cántico completo.

2. Toque un instrumento.
   Solicite a un músico que toque su instrumento para compartir la melodía de un cántico, solamente instrumental. Pida al grupo que identifique cuál es y relacione con el tema.

3. Relacione el texto con un género musical.
   Pida que escojan el texto que prefieran. Entonces, que lo conecten con la música. ¿Cuál es el género musical que les recuerda el texto?

4. Relacione el texto con algún instrumento musical.
   Pida que escojan el texto que prefieran. Entonces, que lo conecten con un instrumento musical ¿Cuál es el instrumento musical que viene a su mente?
   Relacione la escena que más le impactó con algún instrumento musical.

5. Mencione alguna canción que la enseñanza le recuerde.
   ¿Cuál canción o himno viene a su mente al leer la historia?

6. Identifique los ruidos que pudieron escucharse a través de la historia, por ejemplo: el buen samaritano.

Competencia lógico-matemática

¿Qué es? Es la capacidad de hacer patrones con ideas, de plantearse preguntas, de formar cadenas de razonamiento, de amar la solución de un problema, de comprender las relaciones, similitudes y diferencias, de formular hipótesis científicas y otros procedimientos formales. Es la habilidad para manipular símbolos y palabras, de reconocer problemas significantes y luego resolverlos; la competencia de trabajar con lo abstracto y campos numéricos. Comenzando con observaciones y objetos en el mundo material, el individuo se aproxima a sistemas formales cada vez más abstractos, cuyas interconexiones son cuestiones de lógica en vez de la observación empírica. Los orígenes de la inteligencia lógico-matemática se perciben en las actividades infantiles sobre el mundo físico. Después de los 18 meses de edad, el infante aprecia de modo cabal que los objetos siguen existiendo incluso cuando desaparecen de su vista en un momento dado. Este logro de un sentido de permanencia de objetos constituye una piedra angular para el desarrollo

mental posterior. Luego de que el infante aprecia la permanencia de los objetos, puede pensar y referirse a ellos incluso en su ausencia. También puede apreciar las similitudes entre determinados objetos, a pesar de sus diferencias; por ejemplo, reúne todos los camiones, todos los coches amarillos. Sobre esta base puede hacer agrupamientos, señalando el reconocimiento de una clase o un conjunto. Durante unos cuantos años este reconocimiento carece del aspecto cuantitativo, pero se percata de filas mayores o menores. Las habilidades lógico-matemáticas no se vuelven frágiles como consecuencia de daño cerebral focal, sino más bien como resultado de enfermedades deteriorantes más generales, como la demencia, en las que grandes porciones del sistema nervioso se descomponen con rapidez.

¿Cómo la integramos a la clase? La pregunta es considerada como la más universal de las técnicas (Verdejo y Medina, 2009). Sin embargo, es necesario asegurarnos de hacerla clara y precisa. Si la respuesta a nuestra pregunta es un largo silencio, debemos revisarla. Laura Lee menciona en su artículo *How to increase participation by asking better questions* (2019), que la mayor parte del tiempo estos silencios ocurren por alguna de estas razones: las personas no quieren parecer estúpidas, se sienten intimidadas por quien pregunta, o no quieren arriesgarse a exponer su ignorancia. Las preguntas están clasificadas por el nivel de razonamiento: convergentes y divergentes. Las preguntas convergentes buscan una sola contestación correcta. Recurren a la memoria y estimulan niveles bajos de pensamiento. Por ejemplo, ¿Cómo se llamó el primer rey de Israel? Esta respuesta es dada y no fomenta la reflexión ni la conexión con la vida diaria. En una clase de adultos debe evitarse las preguntas convergentes. En cambio, las preguntas divergentes fomentan el uso de niveles de pensamiento más complejo. Con las preguntas divergentes estimulamos la reflexión con una perspectiva individual y comunitaria, el pensamiento creativo y la diversidad de

planteamientos a partir de las diferencias entre las personas. Las respuestas nos ayudarán a observar cómo está la comprensión del tema y qué necesitamos atender. Algunas actividades son:

1. Pregunta divergente.
   Estimulan el pensamiento creador y los planteamientos diversificados. Permite observar la comprensión y el desarrollo del conocimiento. La respuesta del discípulo puede ayudar al maestro a enfocar la enseñanza.

2. Contraste.
   Presenta situaciones, experiencias, hechos o realidades para comparar condiciones diferentes u opuestas, inquirir, inferir, establecer conexiones y concluir. Entre los conceptos que puede contrastarse están: cultura, gobierno, épocas, países, aspectos físicos, situaciones o conflictos. Por ejemplo, compare la nacionalidad de los tres viajeros que vieron al moribundo. Evalúe la acción del samaritano a favor del judío moribundo.

3. Debate.
   Se reta a los miembros del grupo a que asuman una postura y la defiendan. Pueden crearse dos grupos en clase o de acuerdo al número de presentes. Debe incluirse unas reglas a seguir que consideren, por ejemplo, cuándo cada grupo tendrá la oportunidad de refutar, si es inmediatamente después que el otro grupo exprese su punto de vista o tendrá otro turno.

4. Nota dialéctica.
   Es el diálogo con el texto donde el discípulo analiza y responde al texto. Se selecciona un pasaje importante

de las lecturas de la clase, el discípulo divide el papel verticalmente por la mitad. En la columna izquierda anota sus propios comentarios, acuerdos, desacuerdos y preguntas sobre lo leído. Pasadas una o dos reuniones de clase, volverán a leer el texto y responderán en la columna derecha a lo que escribieron anteriormente.

5. Papel en un minuto.
   Reta a los discípulos a contestar las siguientes preguntas sobre un tema particular: qué, a quién, cuándo, dónde, cómo y por qué. Luego de contestar las preguntas, deben sintetizar las contestaciones en una sola oración.

6. Análisis de caso.
   Se presenta una situación a la que los discípulos deben dar solución utilizando los conocimientos adquiridos en clase.

7. Diálogos inventados.
   Mediante la invención de diálogos, los discípulos sintetizan su conocimiento sobre asuntos, personalidades y periodos históricos, en forma de conversaciones cuidadosamente estructuradas.

8. Análisis de artículos.
   Entregue un artículo y pida que reaccionen a las ideas planteadas en un escrito (individual, en pareja o grupal)

9. Diálogo Socrático.
   Se presenta una pregunta o dilema y el grupo utilizan su experiencia y pensamiento para ofrecer una respuesta o solución.

10. Solución de problemas.
    Conduce a los discípulos a tomar conciencia de cómo ellos resuelven problemas. Explican brevemente cada paso al resolver un problema. Al analizar esta información, los maestros pueden determinar el nivel de destreza de solución de problemas del discípulo.

11. Organizadores gráficos.
    Es una forma de representar visualmente cómo la información se relaciona. Se organizan las ideas como parte de un todo y no como conceptos aislados. Los más utilizados han sido aquellos que expresan relaciones numéricas mediante barras, círculos o líneas. Sin embargo, existen otros que se prestan para usarse con conceptos y si es necesario combinarlos con números u otros símbolos, entre ellos:

    a. Mapas conceptuales: Son representaciones de conceptos, significados y las relaciones entre estos. Expresan una o varias proposiciones del concepto por medio de palabras-enlace, entre ella: de, donde, para, el, entonces, con; además de verbos o sustantivos que sirven para construir las proposiciones que se leen entre los nódulos.
    b. Diagramas de estructuras ramificadas. Se utilizan para representar niveles jerárquicos, tales como los árboles de relevancia y niveles estructurales de función.
    c. Diagramas de flujo. Sirven para ilustrar la sucesión temporal de acontecimientos procedimientos o hechos. Permiten una aproximación lógica y rápida, haciendo uso de símbolos, líneas y palabras que representan la secuencia.

Competencia visual - espacial

¿Qué es? Es la capacidad para percibir el mundo visual, realizar transformaciones y modificaciones a las percepciones iniciales propias. También, recrear aspectos de la experiencia visual propia, incluso en ausencia de estímulos físicos apropiados, y expresarse en forma exclusivamente verbal. Se puede pedir a la persona que produzca formas o que tan sólo manipule las que se han proporcionado. Un individuo puede ser agudo en la percepción visual, tener buen recuerdo visual, pero poca habilidad para dibujar, imaginar o transformar el mundo ausente. A menudo es conocida como el pensamiento visual-espacial. Sin embargo, puede desarrollarse también en un individuo ciego, que por tanto no tiene acceso directo al mundo visual, pues tiende a convertir las experiencias espaciales en el número de pasos seguidos en determinada dirección. Por ejemplo, plantear tareas análogas en la modalidad táctil, lo mismo para ciegos que para videntes, proveerles reglas que faciliten el grado de articulación y precisión en el dibujo.

¿Cómo la integramos a la clase? Hacer un dibujo para representar visualmente la enseñanza bíblica nos ayudará a retenerla en nuestra mente para vivirla y compartirla. Danii Marín nos comparte en su libro Dibuja tu fe cómo logró vencer el aburrimiento, la confusión, la distracción y el olvido que le impedían conectarse con la Palabra de Dios (Marín, 2019). Confiesa que tomar notas no le ayudaba, porque después de un rato perdía su atención. Además, luego no revisaba las notas, y si lo hacía, no recordaba por qué había escrito lo que escribió ni su letra era legible. Entonces, decidió como estrategia personal para entenderla, retenerla y vivirla la representación visual. Marín define dibujar como describir de forma visual una idea que se ve o se piensa. Señala que la forma visual también se aplica si solo damos jerarquía a los términos o palabras; nos enseña otras

técnicas como las líneas conectoras, las flechas, los contenedores, las viñetas (bullets), los colores y sombras, entre otras. Al igual que el Dr. Gardner, cree que todos tenemos la capacidad de comunicarnos visualmente, solo hay que practicarlo. Nos anima diciendo que los beneficios de los dibujos no están reservados para los artistas con un talento innato para dibujar, sino para todos. Explica que podemos dibujar casi todo usando cinco figuras geométricas (rectángulo, círculo, triángulo, punto y línea) como alfabeto visual.

1. Dibujo.
   Escoja la escena que más le llamó la atención. Dibuje lo que interpreta para su vida.
   Haga un dibujo para representar la enseñanza que recibió.
   Visualice la lectura y dibuje lo que ve. Por ejemplo, piense en el moribundo solo junto al camino, ¿qué ve? Dibújelo.
   Ilustre con un diagrama el orden de la aparición de los personajes en la historia. Seleccione el que más le impactó, escribiendo la razón.

2. Tirillas cómicas.
   Combine lo verbal con lo pictórico para expresar su interpretación de la lectura, o el mensaje que Dios le da. Dibuje el personaje con detalles que reflejen cómo se siente y cómo se ve.

3. Proyecte el texto clave.
   Pida a la clase que represente su mensaje de manera visual, ya sea con dibujo, palabras o su combinación.

4. Proyecte una diapositiva en blanco.
   Entregue un papel en blanco. Pida que ilustre con creatividad lo que aprendió o el mensaje que recibió en clase.

5. Dibuje o proyecte un mapa geográfico.
   Pida que dibujen la escena que describe el texto. Por ejemplo: Lea el Salmo 23.4 y dibuje lo que allí se describe. (Recordarán mejor el texto luego de fijarse en los detalles porque tienen que dibujar. Esperamos que ninguno se imagine solo en esa escena tenebrosa, de oscuridad, y dibuje al Pastor, quien siempre está presente).

6. Organigrama gráfico.
   Represente las ideas del mensaje, asignándole una ubicación de jerarquía de acuerdo a las prioridades que creemos.

7. Collage.
   Consiste en presentar visualmente un concepto, una idea, un principio o un tema pegando recortes de distintos colores, figuras, tamaños, texturas y tipo, de manera que formen una constelación sobre impuesta. Puede utilizarse individualmente o en grupo. Se necesita tijeras, papel, pegamento, crayones, marcadores, láminas de revistas o periódicos, cintas de colores, escarcha, regla y cualesquiera otros materiales que aporten a la creatividad.

8. Uso de la pizarra.

9. Presentación de la clase en PowerPoint.

Competencia corporal - cinética

¿Qué es? Es la capacidad de usar el cuerpo para fines funcionales o expresivos, y la de trabajar hábilmente con objetos, tanto como los que comprenden los movimientos motores finos de los dedos y manos, como los movimientos motores gruesos del cuerpo. El uso corporal se puede diferenciar en una variedad de formas. *¿Cómo la integramos a la clase?*

1. Dramatizar el texto, Pantomima.
   Por ejemplo, actúe como reaccionó el samaritano cuando vio al moribundo.

2. Expresar el texto con el cuerpo.
   ¿Qué expresión corporal representa lo que sintió al leer la historia bíblica?

3. Use marionetas.

4. Represente algún deporte.
   Por ejemplo, use una bola de plástico para arrojarla a quien invite a responder o participar en clase.

5. Escultura en plasticina.
   Entregue plasticina para que representen cómo se sienten con la creación de alguna figura. Déjelo a su imaginación.

6. Hacer alguna manualidad.

7. Simulaciones. Grupos de discípulos crean escenas vivientes o modelos de procesos para demostrar cuánto saben sobre determinado tema

Competencia interpersonal

¿Qué es? Es la capacidad de conocerse a uno mismo para el desarrollo de los aspectos internos de la persona, el acceso a la propia vida sentimental, sus afectos o emociones. Es la capacidad para efectuar al instante discriminaciones entre estos sentimientos —distinguir un sentimiento de placer y uno de dolor; de involucrarse más en una situación o de retirarse de ella— y utilizarlos como un modo de comprender y guiar la conducta propia; de tener la disposición para enfrentar los dolores y las realidades de la existencia humana.

Luego de 10 años de presentar su Teoría, el Dr. Gardner expresó haber modificado en cierta forma sus ideas acerca de la inteligencia intrapersonal. En su libro Estructuras de la mente (1983) hizo hincapié en el grado en que la inteligencia intrapersonal crecía y se organizaba a partir de la vida sensorial del individuo. Luego, señaló lo importante que es contar con un modelo viable de uno mismo y poder recurrir a él en el momento de tomar decisiones acerca de la vida personal (Gardner, 2017). Cada persona puede lograr un elevado grado de competencia en un medio hostil (realidad social) y mostrar un comportamiento inteligente. *¿Cómo la integramos a la clase?*

1. Escuchar a otro.
   La persona compartirá al grupo algún pensamiento o testimonio relacionado al tema de estudio. Por ejemplo, reflexionando sobre la acción del samaritano, ¿cómo actuaría en su lugar? Expresar al grupo los sentimientos que experimentó al escuchar una historia bíblica.

2. Informe oral breve.
   Asigne la investigación de un tema con antelación a la clase. La persona compartirá sus hallazgos frente a la clase y el grupo lo escuchará.

3. La entrevista. Consiste en la interacción conversacional planificada entre dos o más personas. Esta técnica es utilizada para investigar más sobre algún tema, recurriendo a diversas fuentes. Asigne a una o dos personas unas preguntas ya elaboradas (entrevista estructurada), o que escriba sus propias preguntas, para entrevistar algún recurso que sea experto en el tema estudiado o que tenga mayor conocimiento que el de otras personas por su práctica relacionada. También, dele a escoger que formulen sus propias preguntas. En este caso, la entrevista será una tarea asignada para informar en una próxima clase.

4. Sociodrama.
   Los discípulos personifican a uno o más individuos en una representación espontánea de una situación, tal como ellos la perciben. La presentación será de algunos pocos minutos, y se dará por terminada cuando ha ocurrido suficiente acción para dar base a la discusión.

5. Proyecto en grupo.
   Es una tarea de ejecución que ofrece la oportunidad de aplicar la enseñanza y utilizar las destrezas y habilidades del discípulo. También permite asumir responsabilidad, tomar decisiones y satisfacer el interés particular que lo motivó. Requieren de una amplia gama de competencias, son interdisciplinarios y requieren iniciativa y creatividad de parte del discípulo. Puede realizarse de manera individual o grupal (dos o más). Contiene un tema o problema (debe ser un reto) que sirva para organizar las actividades y requiere que se presente el producto del proyecto (por ejemplo, un informe oral, un objeto, etc.).

6. Orar por alguien, orar en grupo, orar al unísono.

Competencia intrapersonal

¿Qué es? Es la capacidad de conocer a otros y relacionarse con la comunidad exterior. Es la habilidad de notar y establecer distinciones entre otros individuos, entre sus estados de ánimo, temperamentos, motivaciones e intenciones. En su forma elemental, es la capacidad del infante para discriminar entre los individuos a su alrededor y para descubrir sus distintos estados de ánimo. En forma avanzada, es la capacidad del adulto para leer las intenciones y los deseos, aunque estén escondidos, de otros individuos y actuar con base en ese conocimiento. Así el adulto influye en un grupo de individuos dispares para que se comporten según la dirección deseada. *¿Cómo la integramos a la clase?*

1. El autorretrato.
   Es la descripción o enumeración de las características de una persona elaborada por sí misma. Es un perfil de cómo se ve la persona en el presente. Puede crearse de manera diversa: fotos, acróstico, adjetivos, dibujos y la combinación de estos.

2. Diario reflexivo.
   Esta técnica es para uso personal y opcional. Se orienta al discípulo a reflexionar y escribir sobre sus conceptos, sentimientos y actitudes experimentadas al efectuar una tarea o sobre la enseñanza recibida. El discípulo tiene la oportunidad de autoanalizarse y autoevaluarse por medio de unas preguntas guías que se le ofrecen. Esta reflexión puede originar otras preguntas que el discípulo podrá traer a clase, de manera que le ayude a clarificar los conceptos discutidos.

3. Récord anecdótico.
   Consiste en escribir una descripción breve y objetiva en relación con un incidente o comportamiento del cual se es testigo. Se utiliza como técnica en el comportamiento observado. El discípulo puede visitar una sinagoga y anotar lo que observa. Luego en clase, puede utilizarse la observación anotada como inicio de discusión del tema. El formato del record puede contener un mínimo de información: quien se observó, la fecha del incidente u observación y la descripción de lo observado.

4. Lectio Divina.
   Una disciplina espiritual para la lectura bíblica de cuatro pasos: Leer, Meditar, Orar, y Actuar. Presente la cita bíblica y los pasos a seguir con unas preguntas claves que el discípulo debe contestar. Esta dinámica puede ser individual o de manera comunitaria, congregacional.

   Paso 1: Leer, ¿Qué dice el texto bíblico?
   Paso 2: Meditar, ¿Qué dice el Señor?
   Paso 3: Oración, ¿Qué me hace decir al Señor el texto bíblico?
   Paso 4: Actuar, ¿Qué debo vivir (hacer) según el texto bíblico?

Competencia naturalista

¿Qué es? Es la capacidad de detectar, diferenciar y categorizar los aspectos vinculados al entorno, como por ejemplo las especies de animales y vegetales o fenómenos relacionados con el clima, la geografía o los fenómenos de la naturaleza. Es un reflejo de nuestra capacidad de aprender acerca de todo tipo de entornos y de interactuar adecuadamente con los elementos que hay disponibles

en ellos. Inicialmente las capacidades de esta competencia eran incluidas en la inteligencia espacial y lógico-matemática. Sin embargo, tras investigar acerca de ella y los diversos aspectos que la conforman, decidió considerarla y reconocerla como una inteligencia independiente y diferenciada. Incluye las habilidades, tales como: observación, experimentación, reflexión y cuestionamiento de nuestro entorno, sensibilidad y orientación hacia la naturaleza, adaptación a diferentes entornos, coleccionismo de elementos naturales. La poseen en alto nivel los botánicos, cazadores, ecologistas, los paisajistas, quienes aman los animales, quienes aman las plantas, a quienes les gusta investigar las características del mundo natural y del hecho por el ser humano, entre otros (Gardner, 2006; Maldonado, 2008). *¿Cómo la integramos a la clase?*

1. Lectura para relacionar con el entorno natural.
   Describa el entorno natural que relaciona con la lectura bíblica. Explique por qué pensó en ese entorno.
   Dibuje el entorno natural que relaciona con la lectura bíblica. Explique por qué pensó en ese entorno.

2. Observación. Observa el cielo. Escribe los textos bíblicos que te recuerda.

3. Preparación para el estudio en el entorno natural.
   Recomiende que realicen la lectura de preparación para el próximo estudio bíblico (asignación) en un entorno natural; por ejemplo, en una noche bajo las estrellas, en la playa, entre otras.

4. Crear un pequeño huerto (frutos o flores).
   Este puede ser un proyecto de grupo (en la casa o en los terrenos del templo) para demostrar su aprecio por el

regalo de la naturaleza y el llamado a la buena administración de ella.

PLAN DE CLASE

El plan de clase es la organización que dirige la planificación y presentación. Es la guía que redactamos de la manera que nos resulte más útil, donde se organiza la enseñanza en secuencia y se identifican las actividades que determinamos para cumplir su propósito, distribuyendo el tiempo de clase para asegurar su viabilidad. Hoy se dice que la buena enseñanza requiere una conciencia de todos los componentes para aprovechar las oportunidades, anticipar y abordar los desafíos: conciencia del yo como maestro, conciencia del proceso de enseñanza, conciencia del alumno, conciencia de la interacción y conciencia del contexto (Rodríguez & Fitzpatrick, 2014).

A continuación la descripción de los tres pasos para la clase bíblica como una guía para su planificación.

Paso 1: Inicio

¿Cómo logro el interés del discípulo? La actividad de motivación y el propósito son el contenido de este paso, que compartiremos de manera creativa para despertar el interés de quienes escuchan, activar su curiosidad. Este inicio es clave por dos razones: compartiremos una enseñanza que todos necesitamos y lo comunicaremos de una manera convincente. Esto tenemos que hacerlo en un tiempo sin dilatación, pues podríamos perder la atención voluntaria que corresponde a la expectación del inicio. Este paso tendrá un máximo de 15% del tiempo de clase.

Tomemos como ejemplo una clase con el tema del dominio propio. La actividad de inicio será la lectura de una estrofa del poema ¿Y tu agüela, aonde ejtá?, del poeta puertorriqueño Fortunato Vizcarrondo. Si tenemos en clase alguien con voz de locutor o locutora, coordinamos previamente para que haga la lectura a todo el grupo, según la vemos en la Figura 5. Integremos la tecnología disponible, como un proyector digital, pizarra electrónica u otra. Esta actividad de ejemplo usa la competencia lingüística, interpersonal y espacial.

Figura 5: Poema

¿Y tu agüela, aonde ejtá?

Ayé me dijite negro
Y hoy te boy a contejtá:
Mi mai se sienta en la sala.
¿Y tu agüela, aonde ejtá?
Aquí el que no tiene dinga
Tiene mandinga . . ¡ja, ja!

Fortunato Vizcarrondo, poeta puertorriqueño (1942)

¿Por qué usar este poema? Porque su título es conocido por muchos en Puerto Rico y fuera de Puerto Rico y es repetido de manera cotidiana. Entonces fomentaremos la participación para responder cuándo se utiliza esa frase y su significado, de modo que los ejemplos mencionados lo vincularían con nuestro contexto de vida y su conexión demostraría la pertinencia del tema a estudiar. (Esta es una expresión colonial que se utiliza además del contexto con tema racial—por el cruce de razas entre sangre indígena y africana—en otras direcciones para ilustrar con igual exactitud lo que el autor quiere hacer notar: que no somos perfectos 100%). Un ejemplo como éste será una dinámica rompe hielo, de integración y compartir coloquial.

Entonces, articulamos nuestro ejemplo con el propósito mediante una oración conectora como: esta clase es importante para cada uno de nosotros porque el que no tiene dinga, tiene mandinga. Entonces leemos el propósito, que también podríamos proyectar como vemos en la Figura 6.

Figura 6: Propósito

Propósito
Reconocer que necesito practicar el dominio propio con el poder de Dios para disfrutar de una vida abundante.

El propósito debe tener relevancia y sentido de inmediatez para los discípulos. Lo informaremos al inicio de la clase para darle dirección. Podría ser solo una oración que informe de manera clara lo que Dios desea enseñarnos y nuestra acción para integrar la enseñanza a la vida diaria. Si el recurso bíblico (por ejemplo: revista, expositor) ya tiene un propósito, vamos a revisarlo para identificar si es necesario hacer alguna paráfrasis con el fin de asegurar sea significativo a nuestra realidad de vida con una aplicación viable.

En nuestro tiempo de preparación buscamos entender cuál es el propósito de Dios de cada clase. En esa dinámica personal aprovechamos para escribir todas aquellas oraciones sencillas que nos parecían ser un propósito claro. Sin embargo, luego que completemos la estrategia de enseñanza en la planificación, regresaremos a mirar el propósito para asegurar su pertinencia y dirección de la enseñanza. Aquí radica la esencia de nuestra tarea de mayordomía, de servir el don de Dios como buenos administradores. Recordemos que la enseñanza bíblica tiene que estar clara y ser útil para nosotros; si no lo está ni vemos su utilidad personal, falta lo más importante antes de enseñar: tener nuestro encuentro personal con Dios.

Paso 2: Desarrollo

¿Cómo lo voy a hacer? Las actividades de estudio bíblico, de aplicación y de autoevaluación son el contenido de este paso. Este paso tendrá un máximo de 70% del tiempo de clase.

Articulemos la orientación con el propósito de la clase. ¿Cuál será la dinámica de la clase para cumplir el propósito? ¿Cuál es la estrategia que usaremos para provocar la participación y conectar con el texto bíblico para reflexionar sobre el mensaje a nuestra vida que nos dirija a responder con la acción? Con el propósito de identificar algunos ejemplos sobre el contenido de este paso, enumeramos las actividades. Esto no significa que solo usemos una actividad para la dinámica del estudio bíblico, la aplicación y la autoevaluación.

Actividad 1

Ya sabemos que los recursos son apoyo para nuestra preparación y planificación. También podemos realizar una actividad tecnológica en cualquier momento de la presentación. Por ejemplo, usemos la aplicación de la Biblia de YouVersion (www.bible.com, youversion.com) para aprender más sobre lo que significa esperanza, según diversas versiones de la Biblia. Descubrirán que la Traducción en Lenguaje Actual la define como la seguridad de que él cumplirá sus promesas. Esta actividad resultará muy útil para fomentar el aprendizaje activo; además, fomentará el interés por consultar diversas versiones bíblicas para una mejor comprensión del texto cuando realizan su estudio personal. La Figura 7 demuestra cómo asignar esta actividad.

Figura 7: La tecnología como recurso para el aprendizaje activo

Actividad 1: ¿Qué significa esperanza?

Si su celular tiene internet y la aplicación www.bible.com

1. Busque el texto 1 Corintios 13.13
2. Toque el texto para subrayarlo
3. Oprima "Compare"
4. Incluya (+) las versiones: RVR1960, NVI, DHH94, TLA

Las actividades pueden integrar la tecnología con la búsqueda en Internet, ya sea que los discípulos usen su celular o que nosotros la realicemos usando la computadora en una proyección digital. El uso de la Internet es uno de los recursos de la educación ante la trasformación tecnológica, lo cual nos presenta un gran reto. El informe de EducationSuperHighway de los Estados Unidos, declaró en octubre de 2019 que el 99% de las escuelas a nivel nacional tienen acceso a la Internet. El 87% de los maestros de toda la nación dicen que usan el aprendizaje digital en su salón de clases varias veces en la semana. El 96% de los maestros y administradores creen que el aprendizaje digital tiene un impacto positivo en la efectividad del instructor y los resultados de los estudiantes.[19] La realidad es que la mayoría de nuestros discípulos, especialmente los jóvenes, vienen con expectativas altas sobre la presentación de una clase; esto por su experiencia con la tendencia actual de la educación en el ambiente académico o su educación continua laboral.

Alyson Klein compartió en Education Week el tema del impacto de las grandes compañías tecnológicas en las salas de clases, tales como: Amazon, Apple, Google y Microsoft (Klein, 2020). Estas invierten millones en K-12 a través de filantropías. Además, Microsoft y Google crean productos solo para escuelas y los regalan de forma gratuita. Esa presencia en K-12 no es bien recibida por muchos educadores, algunos de los cuales ven a estas compañías como malos vecinos con poca consideración por las verdaderas necesidades de las escuelas. Así lo demostró una encuesta nacional representativa de los docentes, donde el 60 por ciento de los maestros en EEUU están preocupados porque esas Big Tech tienen una gran influencia en las escuelas K-12. Los analistas del mercado dicen que esa actividad no se trata de una ganancia sustancial monetaria, sino más bien de una inversión en el futuro de

19. 2019 State of the States Report. ©2019 EducationSuperHighway.

trabajadores como el de clientes. Esto porque quieren asegurarse de que su sistema operativo, todo su ecosistema, se arraigue realmente en la vida de los estudiantes. A esta crítica, los representantes de las cuatro compañías tecnológicas descartaron la idea de que estaban en el mercado K-12 principalmente para llegar temprano con la próxima generación de usuarios.

Ciertamente la tecnología tiene sus ventajas y facilita algunas de las funciones educativas si tenemos el recurso disponible. Sin embargo, esto no sustituye nuestra creatividad ni cancela la diversidad de recursos que apoyan nuestra tarea para enfocar la clase con efectividad. Se dice que la creatividad es la inteligencia de los sentidos, lo que nos brinda un torrente de opciones (Goleman, 1995). Entonces, estamos claro que la tecnología no define la clase, sino que es un recurso que podría facilitarnos la tarea educativa siempre y cuando sea viable. Los recursos incluyen los materiales, la revista bíblica o expositor bíblico, comentarios bíblicos, diccionarios, instalaciones físicas y tecnológicas, computadora, proyector digital y otros facilitadores o herramientas que sean apoyo para cumplir con nuestra tarea. La figura 8 muestra el ejemplo de una actividad de aplicación.

Figura 8: Actividad de aplicación

Actividad 2: ¿Por qué es feliz quien tiene su esperanza en DIOS?

Lea en silencio el Salmo 146.5-9
y circule la razón que más le guste.

Autoevaluación

La tendencia actual de la educación reconoce la evaluación como parte de la estrategia de enseñanza, pues el propósito más importante de la evaluación no es demostrar, sino perfeccionar (Stufflebeam, 1995). Aunque usualmente en la actividad de aplicación se crea la oportunidad de corroborar si entendieron la enseñanza, aquí tiene otra oportunidad de hacer alguna pregunta a base del contenido del propósito, para corroborar si logramos el mismo. De otra manera, estamos a tiempo para afirmar la enseñanza. Luego, nos referimos al momento de reflexión personal (autoevaluación) para determinar cuál es nuestro estado actual ante la demanda de la enseñanza. Pida que identifique lo que necesita corregir o aplicar en su vida y que lo escriba para compartirlo con Dios en oración. También, podría dar una pregunta o una encuesta breve. Por ejemplo, en una clase donde se estudió la Bondad como fruto del Espíritu, podemos usar una encuesta sencilla como demuestra la Figura 9.

Figura 9: Autoevaluación sobre mi práctica de la bondad

Autoevaluación

Valore cómo se encuentra hoy su BONDAD, siendo el 1 de menor valor y el 10 el valor superior.

1	2	3	4	5	6	7	8	9	10

Paso 3: Cierre

¿Cómo los comprometo con su aprendizaje, con su transformación? La asignación y la oración final son el contenido de este paso. Este paso tendrá un máximo de 15% del tiempo de clase. Vea ejemplo en la Figura 10.

Asignación

La asignación nada tiene que ver con rendir cuentas de sí la hizo o no la hizo, de otorgar puntuación o reconocimiento alguno. Esa dinámica es individual, entre Dios y la persona. A nosotros nos toca ser buen servidor de la gracia de Dios y dirigirlo a entender que la enseñanza no termina cuando finaliza el tiempo de la clase, sino que continúa para llevarnos a la acción. Después de la enseñanza imitamos al Maestro como dijo cuando terminó la parábola del buen samaritano: Ve y haz tú lo mismo.[20]

Integramos la asignación a la clase para fomentar la práctica de la enseñanza del día, para vivir la verdad y crecer en su amor.[21] Por tanto, diseñamos la asignación con doble propósito:

1. una tarea que nos lleve a la aplicación de la enseñanza para vivir la espiritualidad cristiana en todas las relaciones (con Dios, consigo mismo, con los demás y con la naturaleza);
2. la lectura bíblica para la preparación del próximo estudio y para promover el compromiso continuo con nuestro crecimiento espiritual y nuestra transformación.

Figura 10: Asignación

Asignación

- Demuestra un acto de bondad esta semana a quien se lo debes.
- Lea Génesis 39.1-6 y Lucas 1.26-56

¿De dónde viene la idea de incluir la asignación? La demanda en nuestro contexto educativo que la práctica docente comprometa al estudiante con su propio aprendizaje. Aunque la asignación es histórica, en el año 2011 el Departamento de Educación Federal solicitó a las instituciones que reciben fondos federales la revisión de sus programas académicos para incluir la asignación como requisito y rendir cuentas sobre su cumplimiento. Esto tuvo su origen en la creciente protesta de patronos al encontrar que sus

20. Lucas 10.37
21. Efesios 4.15

empleados nuevos contaban con las credenciales o diplomas que evidenciaban su preparación académica, pero no demostraban las competencias requeridas para ejercer la profesión. A estos diplomas se les llamó diplomas de paja. Esta realidad motivó a que se le asignara a la Institución la responsabilidad de asegurar que el estudiante se comprometiera con su propio aprendizaje.[22] Por tanto, la agencia acreditadora busca que ésta cumpla con los requisitos federales de contar con el mínimo de horas de trabajo adicional fuera de clase, utilizando como evidencia la asignación de lecturas para la preparación para la clase y/o algún proyecto o tarea.[23]

En cuanto a la escuela bíblica, fomentamos el encuentro con Dios mediante la asignación de la lectura bíblica. La idea es que aprendamos a reconocer la voz del Maestro y no lo confundamos con el hortelano.[24] Como la lectura bíblica nos motiva a la oración, enseñe que tengan a la mano con qué escribirlo cuando esté leyendo. Además, la asignación de lectura para la preparación del próximo estudio fomentará que el espacio en clase se transforme en un ambiente educativo dinámico e interactivo. Esto porque serviremos como guía en la comprensión del mensaje de Dios mediante el ejercicio práctico en clase, en lugar de dar una conferencia, clase magistral o narrar la historia bíblica. Invertiremos el espacio habitual que usábamos para dar una conferencia, a liderar la comprensión del tema con una dinámica de integración y participación activa, que fomente presentar las dudas para permitir que la enseñanza sea más acertada.

La práctica de invertir el espacio habitual del aprendizaje teórico y práctico se conoce como la clase invertida (Rosa, 2018). La

22. Guidance to Institutions and Accrediting Agencies Regarding a Credit Hour as Defined in the Final Regulations Published on October 29, 2010, Mar 18, 2011. United StatesDepartment of Education, Office of Postsecondary Education. (Gen-11-06).

23. La educación superior fomentan dos horas de estudios fuera de clase por cada hora de enseñanza teórica en el salón.

24. Juan 20.15

clase invertida es una metodología docente consistente en que el alumno trabaje en casa la parte teórica, habitualmente ofrecida como conferencia en clase, para utilizar el tiempo de clase para preguntar, participar activamente y trabajar en grupo.[25] Por ejemplo, la práctica tradicional de la educación formal que usaba el tiempo de clase para el maestro ofrecer una conferencia sobre el tema con una visión grupal, dejando al estudiante como oyente en clase y le asignaba trabajo para la casa. Así, acciones tradicionales que se hacían en casa como ejercicios, solución de problemas o trabajos en grupos, ahora se realizan en clase con la supervisión del maestro. Esta inversión del espacio también produce un cambio en los roles que tradicionalmente asumían en clase el maestro y el estudiante. Este modelo que surgió como enseñanza semipresencial, terminó siendo válido también para la modalidad presencial.

Oración

Utilice una manera diferente en cada clase para realizar la oración final; por ejemplo: individual, en pareja, en cadena grupal, al unísono. Culminemos cada clase afirmando nuestra fidelidad a Dios, la determinación de comprometernos con nuestra transformación y de practicar la enseñanza. Jesús enseñó: el que permanece unido a mí, y yo unido a él, da mucho fruto; pues sin mí no pueden ustedes hacer nada.[26]

MODELO DE PLAN DE CLASE CON INTELIGENCIAS MÚLTIPLES

La Figura 4 presenta un modelo de Plan de Clase como guía para la planificación en tres pasos: *Inicio, Desarrollo* y *Cierre.*

25. El término Inverted Classroom lo asocian al empleo de técnicas similares en todas aquellas disciplinas en las que el docente quiere un acercamiento a temas específicos previos a la clase.

26. Juan 15.5

Figura 4: Modelo de Plan de Clase con Inteligencias Múltiples

Título:	Fecha:
Texto bíblico:	Grupo:
I. Inicio (15% del tiempo)	
• Actividad de motivación: • Propósito:	
II. Desarrollo (70% del tiempo)	
• Actividad de estudio bíblico: • Actividad de aplicación: • Evaluación/Autoevaluación:	
III. Cierre (15% del tiempo)	
• Asignación: 1. 2. • Oración:	
Marque (√) la diversidad de actividades que usará en clase	
☐ Corporal	☐ Lingüística
☐ Espacial	☐ Lógica
☐ Interpersonal	☐ Musical
☐ Intrapersonal	☐ Naturalista

La correspondencia del modelo a la propuesta de uso de las inteligencias múltiples se demuestra con el uso de varias (cantidad) actividades diversas (diferentes) para promover la interacción, en lugar de dar una conferencia. Usemos la lista de cotejo que menciona las competencias en la parte posterior de la guía para revisar la diversidad. Por ejemplo, procure que cada clase empiece con una actividad diferente, intercambiando las competencias. Aseguremos. Solamente la autoevaluación es una actividad intrapersonal ya dada, pues se trata de una reflexión individual y privada.

Cada paso recomienda un por ciento aproximado del tiempo de la clase, de manera que hagamos nuestro propio cálculo. Mantener la conciencia del tiempo ayudará en asegurar su buen manejo y ajuste si surgiera alguna dinámica en clase no proyectada previamente. Como dice el Dr. Gardner, nos toca hacer la tarea con sabiduría y en forma productiva, con la conciencia de lo que estamos haciendo (Gardner, 2017).

PRESENTACIÓN EN POWERPOINT COMO GUÍA

Es de gran ventaja trabajar nuestro plan de clase en una presentación de PowerPoint. La creación de un formato en PowerPoint nos facilitará nuestra tarea para cada clase. Ésta es una herramienta informática de apoyo creada por Microsoft para realizar presentaciones creativas con el fin de facilitar la exposición de un tema. Su contenido es sencillo y fácil de comprender. El presentador no hará lectura de las diapositivas, sino interpretará lo que aparece reflejado en la pantalla, de manera que pueda mantener el contacto visual con el grupo.

Una presentación efectiva requiere presentar el contenido necesario, en la secuencia correspondiente; distinguiendo cada sección de manera clara y llamativa por el cambio de letra, color o incluyendo alguna imagen. Una presentación en PowerPoint tiene otras ventajas que podemos aprovechar, como la de ver las notas del presentador que necesitamos recordar, pero que no deseamos que se vean en la proyección. Aquí solo incluimos aquello esencial; ciertamente pretendemos motivar su búsqueda para conocer mejor este recurso. Por ejemplo, entre las recomendaciones para diseñar la presentación en PowerPoint se encuentran:[27]

- Usar siempre márgenes.
- Utilizar letras leíbles como Arial, Calibri, Tahoma, Times New Roman, Verdana; con un tamaño mínimo para los títulos de 22 pts. y el cuerpo de 16pts.
- Escribir no más de 5 líneas de texto por diapositiva.
- Utilice el contraste de color asegurando su legibilidad.
- Incluir solo un máximo de dos ideas en cada diapositiva.
- Utilizar un elemento visual por diapositiva y que sea novedoso/original. Si fuera el caso de una comparación, no utilizar más de cuatro.
- Alinear a la izquierda los textos en lugar de justificar.
- Evitar animaciones porque distraen. Si fuera necesario algún efecto, "aparecer" o "desaparecer" serán suficientes.
- Evitar utilizar más de cuatro colores en la presentación

27. Marcela Almeida. Guía para elaborar una presentación efectiva en Power Point. Universidad de los Andes. LEO, lectura, escritura y oralidad en español. https://leo.uniandes.edu.co/index.php/oralidad-sec-menu/87-guia-para-elaborar-una-presentacion-efectiva-en-power-point

- No subrayar porque dificulta la lectura. Si necesita dar énfasis, use negrilla.

Después que completemos la presentación de PowerPoint, pongámonos en el lugar de los que la verán. Busquemos identificar aquello que podría confundirnos, nos distrae, no es leíble o no es necesario. Entonces mejoremos la presentación corrigiendo lo que es necesario. Recordemos, es solo una guía, debe ser sencilla y solo necesitará aproximadamente de siete a diez diapositivas.

3

PRESENTACIÓN

"Todo lo que hagan, háganlo para que Dios sea alabado por medio de Jesucristo, a quien pertenece la gloria y el poder para siempre. Amén"

1 PEDRO 4.11

La tercera P está dirigida al día de la clase, cuando nos encontramos frente a los discípulos. Estamos preparados y ya fuimos ministrados por Dios. Proyectamos la confianza de una buena planificación, de tener una guía para dirigir bien la clase y contamos con la ayuda del Espíritu Santo. Entonces falta la experiencia del día, aquello que no se puede conocer con anticipación. Como buenos líderes es necesario observar y escuchar con mucha atención lo que sucede y se expresa para determinar cómo manejarlo. También, la conciencia de que cada acción deberá representar los valores del reino y modelar el carácter de nuestro Maestro, en palabras y hechos. Lo haremos tan bien de forma tal que todos experimentarán el amor de Dios, pues la enseñanza tiene el amor como motivo.

Veamos algunos detalles adicionales en cada paso para que este encuentro sea bueno y edificante.

INICIO

Aseguremos que nos escuchan bien en todos los espacios donde se encuentran las personas; primero hagamos una prueba. El inicio de la clase debe ser con fuerza y alegría, que demuestre nuestro interés y gane el interés de ellos. Nuestra actitud o la disposición de ánimo que demostramos, tiene que ser convincente; es un reflejo del encuentro con Dios que experimentamos en la preparación. Nuestro saludo siempre marcará un ambiente ameno cuando inicia con la sonrisa que trasmite la paz de Dios y la experiencia de su amor. El sabio Salomón lo dijo de manera sencilla: Corazón alegre, cara feliz; corazón enfermo, semblante triste.[1] Ciertamente vivimos días buenos y otros no muy buenos; sin embargo, nos referimos a la alegría que produce el Espíritu.[2] Aquella que representa la salud que Dios da en nuestro interior, a pesar de las circunstancias adversas que rodean nuestra vida. Esa sonrisa está acompañada con un tono de voz que refleje el vigor de nuestra convicción de que está con nosotros aquel que ya venció al mundo.[3]

Demos a todos la bienvenida. Reconozcamos a la visita dándole la bienvenida y preguntando su nombre; digamos el nuestro para propiciar un ambiente de confianza e integración. Informemos el tema de enseñanza y la referencia bíblica. Dirijamos una oración por la enseñanza bíblica, si no se hizo antes. Es preferible que la hagamos nosotros, de manera que sea sencilla, breve y afirme la disposición para aprender lo que Dios quiere enseñar, haciendo referencia al tema del día.

Entonces, activemos la curiosidad y el interés por el tema con la actividad de motivación; y que ésta nos lleve con fluidez a presentar el propósito.

---

1. Proverbios 15.13
2. Gálatas 5.22
3. Juan 16.33

DESARROLLO

Es necesario explicar cómo llevaremos a cabo la clase y de qué forma esperamos que participen. Por ejemplo, podemos compartir el orden de los temas a seguir, orientar sobre el tiempo de participación, la integración deseada. Establezcamos expectativas claras y demos tiempo para pensar. Así los discípulos tendrán dirección y facilitaremos su participación. De otra manera, estarán desorientados y con mucha probabilidad algunos se abstendrán con el temor de adelantarse al tema o de no cumplir las expectativas del maestro.

Evitemos escribir en la pizarra antes de comenzar. Una pizarra llena puede ser un recibimiento que genere estrés en algunos al recordarle la clase de primaria o secundaria que menos querían, y eso no ayudará. Tampoco demos la espalda cuando en su momento escribamos. Ubiquémonos de lado, de manera que podamos hacer un contacto visual con el grupo y pueda ver lo que estamos escribiendo. La pizarra es un recurso para apoyar el proceso educativo, no para distraer o captar la atención lejos de lo que realmente importa. Tenemos ante nosotros un grupo de personas que llegaron a encontrarse con Dios. Tal vez consciente o inconscientemente, pero llegaron al espacio sagrado donde todos juntos estamos frente a su majestad, donde nos reunimos como un solo pueblo, al que Dios llama, da forma y emplea (González, 2017).

Como ya dijimos, en nuestra clase bíblica tenemos la representación de los diversos conflictos y necesidades de la sociedad. Aunque conocemos nuestra propia realidad y nos parece que también la de nuestro país, de nuestra iglesia y, quizás, la de algunos discípulos, no conocemos la situación particular de cada discípulo en ese día. Por tanto, es necesario que nos cultivemos y nos formemos a nosotros mismos para mantener una actitud de receptividad y flexibilidad. Receptividad para escuchar la necesidad y responder a ésta con la ayuda del Espíritu Santo. Flexibilidad para no caer en crisis porque nos falta mucho que decir y el tiempo de clase sigue agotándose. Es por esta razón que previamente identificamos cuál es el propósito de la clase, la esencia de la enseñanza, de tal manera que lo llevemos a cabo haciendo el ajuste para que sea viable.

También una actitud de apertura es necesaria porque escucharemos más de una respuesta y no únicamente las que creemos que recibiremos. La respuesta del discípulo nos ayudará a enfocar la enseñanza, pues nos descubrirá las necesidades o áreas pertinentes que requieren la atención. Con mucha probabilidad recibiremos múltiples y diversas apreciaciones del texto, tanto como los discípulos en clase. Además, recibiremos preguntas a nuestras preguntas, lo que requiere una moderación cuidadosa de nuestra parte. La participación activa y creativa de los discípulos enriquecerá la enseñanza con la diversidad de perspectivas más sus experiencias personales que guarden pertinencia con el tema. También existe el riego de perder el enfoque dado a la riqueza del texto y los diversos temas traídos por la participación. Por tanto, mantenga en mente el tema de la clase y su propósito para lograr su enfoque.

Cuidemos de nuestras emociones y la de los demás en clase. Dependiendo de las emociones en que una persona se encuentre ese día, será el tipo de acción que podrá realizar. En la sala de clases, al igual que en cualquier relación entre personas, surgen emociones de distinto tipo en los participantes; algunas que favorecen ciertas acciones y otras que las dificultan. Los estilos de interacción dependen de la distinción que cada uno haga de los otros y de su circunstancia. Tenemos que reconocer que esta distinción tiene que ver con lo que cada uno trae a la mano de sus particulares construcciones de mundo, experiencias, significados, de su propia historia (Ibañez, 2011). Entonces, la percepción de cada persona depende de factores históricos personales, que no podemos suponer ni exigir objetividad. Cuide que alguna persona no monopolice el tiempo de la clase. Nuestra responsabilidad es mantener el control de un ambiente saludable que sea propicio para la interacción, el compromiso y la acción.

Según la nueva visión de la UNESCO, la educación de calidad *fomenta, garantiza y propicia.* En la educación cristiana enseñamos con la conciencia de fomentar y propiciar la transformación, pero sabemos que no podemos garantizarla, puesto que esto requiere un acto voluntario del que recibe la enseñanza. Aunque tenemos la ayuda esencial del Espíritu Santo en todo el proceso, ciertamente toca a cada uno de nosotros tomar las decisiones ante la demanda de Dios y hacer nuestros ajustes individuales a base de la enseñanza bíblica. Por tal razón, valoramos la actividad de aplicación para dirigirnos a entender la enseñanza a nuestra vida.

El proceso educativo nos invita a la concienciación de quiénes somos y quiénes estamos siendo. El escritor bíblico habla de la debilidad humana, que a veces ni siquiera sabemos orar como es debido, que no nos damos cuenta de nuestros propios errores.[4] Entonces, con mucha probabilidad el día de clase tendrá algunos que no saben qué es lo que realmente le está afectando ni qué es lo que quieren. Por tanto, es necesario que la enseñanza bíblica reitere que necesitamos ser guiados por el Espíritu de Dios para ser hijos de Dios.[5]

El sicólogo y educador Carl R. Rogers habló sobre su experiencia de atender personas afectadas por una amplia variedad de problemas personales, que cambiaban en cada una de las entrevistas cuando tenían que identificar cuál era el problema (Roger, 2011).[6]

---

4. Romanos 8. 26-27; Salmos 19.12

5. Romanos 8.14.

6. Roger es reconocido como el padre de la terapia centrada en la persona.

Roger estudió durante un periodo de 10 años las luchas que sus clientes libraban como individuos y las compartió en su libro El proceso de convertirse en persona. Concluyó que quién soy yo es una pregunta que todos necesitamos contestar para crecer y madurar como persona. Señala que las personas esconden conscientemente, detrás de diversas máscaras, sus sentimientos, su mundo interno, sus pensamientos, mostrando una conducta superficial. Roger declara que en el proceso de llegar a ser persona, el individuo acepta que es un proceso de transformación, no un producto ni una entidad estática; aprende a vivir en su vida como quien participa de un proceso dinámico y fluyente, donde el transcurso de la experiencia continua le permite descubrir nuevos aspectos de sí mismo.

La actividad de aplicación nos dará la oportunidad de contestar preguntas para entender la enseñanza. Para nuestro Maestro fue importante conocer el resultado de su enseñanza. Aunque no preguntaran él preguntaba; por ejemplo, Mateo 13.51 dice: Jesús les dijo: habéis entendido todas estas cosas? Ellos respondieron: sí, Señor. La evaluación y la autoevaluación van tomadas de la mano. Es nuestra responsabilidad facilitarlas, dirigiendo a su cumplimiento.

CIERRE

Es nuestra tarea repetir en cada clase cuál es la provisión de Dios y su demanda, siendo propicio en ese momento para fomentar la aceptación de la dirección divina y profundizar más en la fe. Reiterar que nuestra adopción como hijos es un acto de la gracia basado en el amor de Dios.[7] Concienciar que recibimos el Espíritu que nos hace hijos de Dios, y por este Espíritu nos dirigimos

7. Romanos 8.15; Gálatas 4.6; Efesios 1.5

a Dios llamándole Padre.[8] Invitar a todos a que disfrutemos de una relación íntima con Dios, con la confianza que nos dio para acercarnos a él.

La doctrina de la creación no nos habla solo acerca del valor de las cosas y de su relación con Dios. También nos dice algo acerca de quiénes somos como seres humanos (González, 2017). Además del ser humano haber sido creado a la imagen y semejanza de Dios, recibió el aliento de vida directamente de Dios para convertirse en un ser viviente.[9] Entonces la combinación de un cuerpo formado de la tierra y el aliento de vida infundido por la divinidad forma un ser viviente (nefesh jayyah). El ser viviente no se utiliza para designar alguna parte de la persona, sino su totalidad; la idea hebrea es de un ente íntegro, distinto a la griega que propone el alma separa del cuerpo (Voth, 1992). Dicho origen establece que el ser humano depende de Dios para vivir la vida para la cual fue creado, además de darle valor a su existencia e identidad como persona.

Entonces, expliquemos la conexión entre la enseñanza y la asignación, cuando afirmaremos nuestra identidad como hijos de Dios para actuar de acuerdo a lo que somos, practicando su enseñanza. Aquí tenemos una nueva oportunidad para invitar a vivir en amistad con Dios, para experimentar la alegría de los magos de oriente cuando encontraron al Salvador y le rindieron honor con su vida y lo que tenían.

Terminemos con una oración de afirmación de una manera diferente en cada clase, y afirmando que la oración privada, personal

8. La expresión Abba en arameo que significa Padre, solo aparece en el Nuevo Testamento tres veces: Marcos 14.36; Romanos 8.15; Gálatas 4.6. Muchos eruditos bíblicos creen que esta palabra aramea era usada por los hijos, especialmente los más pequeños para dirigirse a sus padres, significando intimidad y una relación especial (Rodríguez y Cortés, 2011).

9. Génesis 1.27; 2.7

con Dios, sigue siendo recompensada.[10] Por lo tanto, reiteramos que aunque el tiempo de la clase termine, no significa que es su final. ¡Ahora comienza la parte práctica, en vivo y a todo color! La pasión que demostremos para seguir al Maestro habla de nuestra vida, nuestra experiencia con él. ¿Cuántos maestros y maestras de escuela bíblica pueden decir como el apóstol Pablo: lo que aprendisteis y recibisteis y oísteis y visteis en mí, esto haced?[11]

10. Mateo 6.6
11. Filipenses 4.9

REFERENCIAS

Alvarado león, Gerardo, E. (2019). *Centennials lucharán por un mejor país*. El Nuevo Día, (18 de agosto de 2019), 4-6.

Álvarez, G. (2018). *Narrativa, experiencia y saber. Apuntes para una comprensión del campo educativo*. Voces de la Educación, 3 (6), 3-15).

Álvarez, Héctor Joel. Md.D. (2006). *Los Hallazgos de las neurociencias y su aplicabilidad a la sala de clases: teoría y práctica*. PR: Ediciones Santillana, Inc.

Bíblica, Inc. (2011). *Los Libros de la Biblia: la Historia del Pacto*. Nueva Versión Internacional®NVI® ©1999 por la Bíblica, Inc.™

Bíblica, Inc. (2011). *Los Libros de la Biblia: Nuevo Testamento*. Nueva Versión Internacional®NVI® ©1999 por la Bíblica, Inc.™

Castillo Silva, F. (2018). Andragogía, andragogos y sus aportaciones. *Voces De La Educación*, 3(6), 64-76.

Córica, J.L., y Dinerstein, P. (2012). *Diseño curricular y nuevas generaciones*. Argentina: Editorial Virtual Argentina. Disponible en: http://editorialeva.net/libros

Deiros, Pablo Alberto. (1992) *Santiago y Judas. Comentario Bíblico Hispanoamericano*. Miami, Florida: Editorial Caribe, Inc.

Frazee, Randy. (2011). *La Historia*. Rediseñado. Miami, Florida: Editorial Vida.

Gardner, Howard, Dr. (2017). *Estructuras de la mente: la teoría de las inteligencias múltiples*. Tercera edición en español. Primera edición en inglés, 1983 y segunda aumentada en 1993. Traducción Sergio Fernández Éverest. México: Fondo de Cultura Económica.

__________________. (2006). *Multiple Intelligences: New Horizons*. Primera edición en inglés, 1993. New York: Basic Books.

__________________. (2000). *A case against spiritual intelligence. The International Journal for the Psychology of Religion*, Volume 10, Issue 1 January 2000, pp. 27-34.

Gardner, H. (1998). *A Reply to Perry D. Klein's "Multiplying the Problems of Intelligence by Eight"*. Canadian Journal of Education/ Revue canadienne de l'éducation, 23(1), 96-102.

Goleman, Daniel. (1995). *Emotional Intelligence*. New York: Bantam Books.

González, Jorge, Th.D. (1998). *Tres meses en la escuela de los Salmos.* Nashville, TN: Abingdon Press.

González, Justo L. Ph.D. (2019). Liderazgo en la historia de la iglesia. En Pagán, Samuel (Ed), *Aviva el don que hay en ti: en torno al desarrollo de un liderazgo transformador en el siglo 21* (pp. 129-167). Bayamón, Puerto Rico: La Iglesia Cristiana (Discípulos de Cristo).

____________________. (2017). Conoce tu fe: Cristianismo para el siglo XXI. *Asociación para la Educación Teológica Hispana (AETH), Orlando, FL.*

____________________. (2003). *Historia de la Reforma: un estudio de los eventos que conllevaron a la Reforma Protestante.* Miami, FL: Editorial Unilit.

____________________. (1997). *Tres meses en la escuela de la prisión.* Nashville, TN: Abingdon Press.

Green, Eugenio (1993). *1 Pedro y 2 Pedro. Comentario Bíblico Hispanoamericano*. Miami, Florida: Editorial Caribe, Inc.

Ibáñez Salgado, Nolfa. (2011). *Aprendizaje-enseñanza: mejora a partir de la interacción de los actores. Educación y Educadores*, 14 (3), pp. 457-474.

Klein, Alyson. (2020). What Are the Big Tech Companies Really After? Education Week, Vol 39(Issue 17), Pages 20-21.

Lee, Laura. (2019). How to Increase participation by Asking better questions. Edutopia, October 24, 2019.George Lucas Educational Foundation.

López, Ediberto, Ph.D. (2003). *Para que comprendiesen las Escrituras: Introducción a los Métodos Exegéticos.* San Juan, PR: Seminario Evangélico de Puerto Rico; Fundación Puerto Rico Evangélico.

Maldonado Villamil, Francisco J. (2008). *Estrategias: Métodos y Técnicas de enseñanza para maestros.* Hato Rey, Puerto Rico: Publicaciones Puertorriqueñas, Inc.

Marín, Danii. (2019). *Dibuja tu fe: Entiende, retén y vive la Palabra de Dios visualmente aunque no sepas dibujar.* Miami, Florida: Editorial Patmos.

Marín, Susana. (2014). Poemario. Disponible en: https://poemario.org/poema-del-renunciamiento/

Marzano, Robert J., Ed.D. (2007). *The Art and Science of Teaching: a comprehensive framework for effective instruction.* Alexandria, Virginia USA: Association for Supervision and Curriculum Development.

Mejías Ortiz, Juan R. (2019). Liderazgo y educación transformadora. En Pagán, Samuel (Ed), *Aviva el don que hay en ti: en torno al desarrollo de un liderazgo transformador en el siglo 21* (pp. 209-212). Bayamón, Puerto Rico: La Iglesia Cristiana (Discípulos de Cristo).

Nales Pérez, Nereida, Ed.D. (2006). *Jesús, mi Maestro: su plan educativo transformador.* Fundación Palabra y Más: San Juan, Puerto Rico.

Ortiz García, Ángel L. Ed.D. (2003). *Diseño y evaluación curricular.* Quinta edición. Río Piedras, PR: Editorial Edil.

Padilla, Alvin, Dr. (2007). *Lucas. Serie conozca su Biblia.* Minneapolis: Augusburg Fortress.

Pagán, Samuel, ThD. (2019). Oísteis que fue dicho: Liderazgo en el Nuevo Testamento. En Pagán, Samuel (Ed), *Aviva el don que hay en ti: en torno al desarrollo de un liderazgo transformador en el siglo 21* (pp. 67-127). Bayamón, Puerto Rico: La Iglesia Cristiana (Discípulos de Cristo) en Puerto Rico.

____________________. (2012). *Jesús de Nazaret: vida, enseñanza y significado.* Barcelona, España: Editorial Clie.

______________________. (2007). *Comentario de los Salmos*. Miami, Florida: Editorial Patmos.

Perspectivas: Revista trimestral de educación comparada (París, UNESCO: Oficina Internacional de Educación), vol. XXIII, nos 1-2, 1993, págs. 289-305. UNESCO: Oficina Internacional de Educación, 1999.

Perspectivas Digitales Puerto Rico. (s.f.). Centroamericana y el Caribe: Un oasis de oportunidades en el mundo digital. Disponible en: thinkwithgoogle.com

Rodríguez, José David y Cortés-Fuentes, David. (2011). *Romanos*. Minneapolis: Augsburg Fortress.

Rodríguez, Vanessa & Michelle Fitzpatrick. (2014). *The Teaching Brain: An Evolutionary Trait at the Heart of Education*. The New Press.

Rogers, Carl R. (2011). *El Proceso de convertirse persona*. Traducción por Lilliana R. Wainberg de On becoming a person, 1961. España: Paidós.

Rosa García, Alfonso. (2018). *Aplicando la clase invertida en empresa, economía y turismo*. Editorial Dykinson.

Real Academia Española: «*Diccionario de la Lengua Española*», 23.ª ed., [versión 23.2 en línea]. https://del.rae.es. [noviembre 2019].

Sociedades Bíblicas Unidas. (1994). *La Biblia de Estudio Dios Habla Hoy: con Deuterocanónicos.* Tercera edición. Estados Unidos de América: Sociedades Bíblicas Unidas.

State of the states. (2019). The classroom connectivity gap is now closed. Retrieved 13 January, 2020, from https://stateofthestates.educationsuperhighway.org/?utm_source=The+Hechinger+Report&utm_campaign=655abc6e4e-EMAIL_CAMPAIGN_FOL_2019_10_23_02_18&utm_medium=email&utm_term=0_d3ee4c3e04-655abc6e4e-322739741#national.

Stufflebeam, Daniel, L. (1995). La evaluación orientada hacia el perfeccionamiento. En *Evaluación sistemática* (pp. 175-232). Barcelona Madrid: Ediciones Paidós.

Verdejo-Carrión, Ada L., Ed.D., y Medina-Díaz, María del R., Ph.D, (2009). *Evaluación del Aprendizaje Estudiantil.* 5ª edición. San Juan, PR: Experts Consultants, Inc.

Zhizhko, Elena. (2018). Las TIC y tutoría virtual en la educación personas jóvenes y adultas en México. *Voces De La Educación*, 3 (6), 204-217.

Wigglesworth, Cindy. (2012). *SQ21: The Twenty-One Skills of Spiritual Intelligence*. New York: SelectBooks, Inc.

Comunícate con la autora:

☎ +1 (787) 219-7329

🖃 dnnales@gmail.com